THE G-FORCES

Gita, Governance, Goodness, Godliness

A. VENKATASUBRAMANIAN

INDIA • SINGAPORE • MALAYSIA

ISBN
Paperback 979-8-89632-775-2
Hardcase 979-8-89699-935-5

Dedication

To

GAUTAMA BUDDHA

[The One Who Showed the 'MIDDLE-PATH']

CONTENTS

PART 2: ADMINISTRATOR READ-UP ESSENTIALS

PART 3: SELF-IMPROVEMENT

FOREWORD

INTRODUCTION

Applying the Teachings of the BUDDHA to our Lives

"Train your mind to see the good in everything.
Positivity is a choice.
The happiness of your life depends on the
quality of your thoughts."

- Gautama Buddha

"(On the difference between LOVE & LIKE)
If there is a flower
If we 'LIKE' it .... we just simply pluck it... without thinking.
But if we 'LOVE" it .... then we are going to take care of it."

- Gautama Buddha

AN INTRODUCTION TO THE BOOK

'THE G-FORCES'

"Life is too Ironic,
It takes SADNESS to know what HAPPINESS is,
NOISE to appreciate SILENCE,
And ABSENCE to value PRESENCE."

- Gautama Buddha

"What you THINK, you BECOME,
What you FEEL, you ATTRACT,
What you IMAGINE, you CREATE."

- Gautama Buddha

"If you truly want to change your life,
You must first be willing to change your mind."

- Gautama Buddha

This book **'The G-FORCES'** has been divided into **THREE Parts**.

The **FIRST PART** of the book starts out with Mahatma Gandhi's prescriptions for humanity as encapsulated by the **'7-Deadly Sins'**.

The **'7-Deadly Sins'** are a 'short and crisp' take on how humanity should best conduct itself to strike that elusive balance without derailing itself. The balance that the Mahatma had prescribed for humanity about a hundred years ago are NOT just relevant in the contemporary context, but are timeless. They capture the constant even as the complexities of human existence and interactions play out in a constantly changing world.

The **SECOND PART** of the book deals with a few **read-up essentials** for an administrator and/or policy maker. The chapters in this section are meant to expand the learnings and horizons of the administrator.

It is hoped that after reading the chapters in Part-II of this book, a policy maker will make enhanced decisions when it comes to policy making. It is hoped that this would create a more positive decision making, that ultimately impacts the population at large.

The **THIRD PART** of the book addresses the relationship between money and happiness. People entrusted with positions of power are meant to be in the service of people. They are supposed to command the respect and love of the populace based on their actions. Such actions are to be much above any personal pecuniary benefit.

This part of the book is meant to help the administrators have an enhanced life by putting the money factor into the right framework. In this way, administrators can find peace, satisfaction, happiness and contentment, BOTH in their professional and personal lives.

The FIRST Part of the Book

"Your thoughts influence your feelings,
Your feelings influence your actions,
Your actions create the life that you live."

- Gautama Buddha

"Your beliefs don't make you a better person,
Your Behaviour does."

- Gautama Buddha

The **FIRST part** of this book attempts a **deep dive** into the **Mahatma's '7-Deadly Sins'.** This part of the book tries to dissect these **maxims** in the contemporary context.

The world maybe changing fast. However, some things still hold and remain a constant even as the rest just keeps moving, changing and reshaping life. The Mahatma's prescriptions are one of such ever-green MAXIMs. These Maxims act as an anchoring for the individuals and society at large even in the midst of constant flux in every other aspect of modern life.

These are still valid even after about a century since the Mahatma had thought, lived, suffered, deeply contemplated and come up with them. The Mahatma did this deep contemplation for his love of humanity.

These maxims are still as applicable in a contemporary context, as they were over one hundred years ago. These are constant and timeless.

It is this deep contemplation on his part that bubbled up in a distilled form as the '7-Deadly Sins' that society should be wary of to avoid getting derailed.

GAUTAMA BUDDHA

(with the MILDDLE-PATH a millennium+ ago)

&

MAHATMA GANDHI

(with the '7-DEADLY SINS' a hundred years ago)

"Everything in your life is a reflection of a
choice you have made.
If you want a different result,
Make a different choice."

- Gautama Buddha

"Three things cannot be long hidden;
the sun, the moon
and the TRUTH."

- Gautama Buddha

In many ways the prescriptions of Mahatma Gandhi are in parallel to what another great soul had prescribed more than a millennium ago. That great soul was Gautama Buddha.

While the Buddha had prescribed what can be best described in TWO words as the 'MIDDLE-PATH', Mahatma Gandhi had defined those same philosophies in the context of the modern world as the '7-DEADLY SINS'.

The '7-DEADLY SINS' while being more specific and defined is still compact enough to address the broad spectrum of dilemmas of modern living. They serve as the guiding light and show us the way in a difficult and increasingly complicated modern world.

Gautama Buddha on the other hand had prescribed the 'MIDDLE-PATH' from his own very deep contemplation of human suffering, happiness, existence and meaning of life. These are more philosophical and generic while acting as the guide over a broader canvas at a deeper philosophical level.

The SECOND Part of the Book

"Be open to everything
BUT
unattached."

- *Gautama Buddha*

"You learn nothing from life
if you think
you are right all the time."

- *Gautama Buddha*

"Most of the problems in life are because of TWO reasons:
1) We act without thinking
Or
2) We keep thinking without acting."

- *Gautama Buddha*

The **SECOND part** of this book deals with what one can call situational awareness that an administrator w.r.t. the way the modern world is moving. This awareness would enable the making of more informed decisions.

"Life is really simple,
but
we insist on making it complicated."

- *Gautama Buddha*

"Sometimes the easiest way to solve a problem
is to
stop participating in it."

- *Gautama Buddha*

This SECOND part consists of '**Chapters**' that are like a **basic tool set**.

These contain **some topics** of interest, that could help a **leader or administrator** make **more informed decisions** in **regard to policy making and implementation**.

The THIRD Part of the Book

"A disciplined mind brings happiness."

- *Gautama Buddha*

"If you are happy at the expense of another man's happiness
you are forever bound."

- *Gautama Buddha*

"Don't be impressed by money, followers, degrees and titles,
be impressed by
kindness, integrity, humility and generosity."

- *Gautama Buddha*

The **THIRD part** of this book consists of '**Chapters**' that are a **must read for any leader or administrator.** These relate to chapters on **finance and philosophy, personal improvement** and **managing one's life better.**

The **THIRD part** of this book is meant to help administrators **gather perspectives** of their **job** and **life** in general in order to better optimally balance their lives and performance on the job.

These it is hoped would lead to **better balance** in their **personal and professional life** while helping administrators **better discharge their duties.**

These chapters **look at money** through the **prism of philosophy**. It helps to look at money and wealth as having many dimensions and components BEYOND the obvious ones.

Actions of a policy maker born out of motivations for pecuniary benefit alone can never lead to better and enhanced outcomes for the individual let alone the society at large.

"HAPPINESS is NOT in
HAVING a lot,
BUT
in GIVING a lot."

- Gautama Buddha

This becomes even more important in case of a policy maker because of the huge power he wields. Hence, wisdom, care and contemplation become even more important.

"The Quieter you become
the more
you can hear"

- Gautama Buddha

CONCLUSION

"To be most successful in life,
always forget the problems
that
you've faced in your life.
But never forget the lessons
that
those problems taught you."

- *Gautama Buddha*

The prescriptions from the **Mahatma** bring us back to **our center and baseline,** while reminding us of the **need to strike a balance,** lest we crash and burn. While these concepts may seem abstract, it is necessary for us to take a step back and **ponder philosophically about human civilization** and where we are taking it.

"Never be a prisoner of your past.
It was just a lesson, NOT a life sentence."

- *Gautama Buddha*

For the actions to be elevated and enhanced, the administrator himself/herself needs to have an elevated understanding of the topic at hand but also needs to be elevated on the spiritual side so that he /she acts in the best interests of his/her populace and humanity as a whole.

"The Secret of health for BOTH the mind and body is
Not to Mourn the past,
Worry about the future, Or anticipate trouble,
BUT
To live in the present moment
WISELY and EARNESTLY."

- *Gautama Buddha*

ACKNOWLEDGEMENT

I would like to thank my **parents, teachers, professors, family**, and
friends who have **taught and challenged me**

to

understand myself and, hence, **understand others better**.

I have since **learnt** that,

'Knowing others is wisdom, but **knowing oneself is self-realization'**.

Having said that,

I would also **like to thank all the other people** who have **touched my life**,

shown me a better way, and, in the process,

made me a **better person,**

while **pushing me towards** my **greatest potential.**

It is **because of their efforts** that,

I have **begun to understand** myself better

and have been able to **approach life** with

a greater **application of wisdom**

rather than,

straight/direct knowledge/ intelligence.

PART I

Deep Dive

into

the

Mahatma's 7-Deadly Sins

INTRODUCTION

The 7 Deadly Sins

"The true civilization is
where every man gives to every other,
every right that
he claims for himself."

- *Robert Green Ingersoll*

"The moment you give up your principles, and your values,
you are dead,
your culture is dead,
your civilization is dead.
Period."

- *Oriana Fallaci*

The 7 Deadly Sins

The more things change, the more they remain the same. In this **constant flux** it would help to recall **what** the **great Mahatma had said**.

With his quote Mahatma Gandhi **helps us center**. He brings us **back to the core values** that would **help humanity survive** and not self-destruct.

I would like to start this book with the **'Seven Deadly Sins'** that he says **individuals and society should be wary of.**

In his words, the **7 Deadly Sins** are:

- **Wealth** without **work,**
- **Pleasure** without **conscience,**
- **Science** without **humanity,**
- **Knowledge** without **character,**
- **Politics** without **principle,**
- **Commerce** without **morality,**
- **Worship** without **sacrifice.**"

The prescriptions from the **Mahatma** bring us back to **our center and baseline,** while reminding us of the **need to strike a balance,** lest we crash and burn. While these concepts may seem abstract, it is necessary for us to take a step back and **ponder philosophically about human civilization** and where we are taking it.

Afterall, we
DEFINE OUR FUTURE
by our
ACTIONS IN THE PRESENT.

While these concepts may seem abstract, it is necessary for us to take a step back and **ponder philosophically about human civilization** and where we are taking it. In the face of the barrage of change and changing times, **we should not be swept so far away from our moorings** that we begin to drift without direction and purpose.

Hence, **no matter the challenges,** our leaders (whether political, societal, religious or corporate) **should NOT shed these core principles. Disregarding these core principles** would **only lead to a path** of **self-destruction.** Hence, disregarding these guidelines is **NOT an Option.**

Placing these principles at the center of what we do, will allow for a **society to be harmonious** and for **all humanity** to have a **fair opportunity to thrive and prosper**, and do so in balance.

I would hence would like to start this book with this introduction to the '7-**Deadly Sins**' and with a deep dive into the same in the **FIRST part** of this book.

It is hoped that these **PRESCRIPTIONS FOR HUMANITY** by the **MAHATMA** would be kept in view at all times as we go about our lives,

as **Individuals, as a Society,**

and

as Humanity.

Chapter 1

WHY CAN'T THERE BE WEALTH WITHOUT WORK?

Wealth is a product of Work, whether it is Labour put in, Knowledge applied, Innovation created, Invention found or a person's Ingenuity & Enterprise

---

"Wealth, like happiness is never attained when sought after directly,
It comes as a by-product of providing a useful service."

- Henry Ford

"Striving for Success without Hard Work is like trying to Harvest
where you HAVEN'T planted."

- David Bly

WEALTH

Questions Posed:

1) Why would **WEALTH** be **PRIMARILY** about ***WORK***?
   a) Why can't **WEALTH** be MORE about ***SACRIFICE*** than about ***WORK***?
   b) Why can't **WEALTH** be MORE about ***MORALITY*** than about ***WORK***?
   c) Why can't **WEALTH** be MORE about ***PRINCIPLES*** than about ***WORK***?
   d) Why can't **WEALTH** be MORE about ***CHARACTER*** than about ***WORK***?
   e) Why can't **WEALTH** be MORE about ***HUMANITY*** than about ***WORK***?
   f) Why can't **WEALTH** be MORE about ***CONSCIENCE*** than about ***WORK***?

a) Why can't WEALTH be MORE about *SACRIFICE* than about *WORK*?

Fundamentally, the way the Universe is designed is that it is a 'Give and Take'. Humans collectively need to put in the work required for basic living including for food, clothing and shelter.

It is a different story that humans have improved living conditions by their ingenuity, thereby increasing the productivity, and thereby the output produced. But this still involved innovation and enterprise (which was work), and also effort needed to maintain and improve from there on.

SACRIFICE in this context, is nothing but expecting that someone would do the work of wealth creation and give its' fruits on a platter to the rest. The reason that won't work, is that often people who talk about sacrifices (to be made for society) are rarely the ones making the sacrifice (from their side) and doing the work.

Also, such a system is in no way a fair or sustainable system. **WEALTH** needs the 'input of work' for its' creation or even existence. Hence, it should be obvious that if one sidelines the focus on work and hopes to be wealthy, we are more likely to sit around and wait for someone else to do the work (to create comfort and wealth for us). This sounds more like socialism and a utopian illusion.

Any society that does NOT respect a good work ethic, does not dignify labor (doesn't uphold dignity of labor), does not prize innovation and does NOT respect hard/smart work is never going to be wealthy. Expecting someone else to come forward and do the work for us, is never a feasible or practical proposition.

b) Why can't WEALTH be MORE about *MORALITY* than about *WORK*?

c) Why can't WEALTH be MORE about *PRINCIPLES* than about *WORK*?

To create **WEALTH**, one needs ***WORK*** as an input. If a society/individual wants to be rich and wealthy, the society/individual needs to put in the work and take the initiative.

There is nothing more ***MORAL*** or ***PRINCIPLED*** about the fact that the wealth should accrue to the person putting in the effort, work and innovation. So, rather than getting side-tracked by other such propositions, a society should promote a meritocracy where the person doing the work should be suitably rewarded.

If one needs to maximize the wealth produced by society one needs to first have a meritocracy (ahead of other ***MORAL*** or ***PRINCIPLE*** based arguments). The simple reason is that if one takes away MERIT or the incentives (such as wealth as a reward) there will be sub-optimal wealth creation for society. Basically, there would be less for everyone and everyone would be worse-off.

When we talk in reference to **WEALTH,** the primary input has to be foremost ***WORK***. The rest can follow, but ***WORK*** as the primary input is a must.

d) Why can't WEALTH be MORE about *CHARACTER* than about *WORK*?

e) Why can't WEALTH be MORE about *HUMANITY* than about *WORK*?

f) Why can't WEALTH be MORE about *CONSCIENCE* than about *WORK*?

When one talks about WORK as being the 'PRIMARY' driver (and ahead of ***MORALS***, ***PRINCIPLES*** and ***CHARACTER***), one is NOT sideling the importance of these other characteristics.

However, just being ***PRINCIPLED*** and having upright ***CHARACTER*** does not automatically cause the plantations to grow, goods to be manufactured or services to be rendered by magic. Similarly, just being a ***HUMANITARIAN*** or having a solid ***CONSCIENCE*** cannot create wealth.

Wealth-creation fundamentally requires hard work. This hard work can be multiplied by organized capital, labor and training, which then can fuel productivity. When innovation, R&D, inventiveness and creativity are added to the mix, these lead to the creation of exponential wealth. However, they do require significant learning, skilling, hard work, smart work and organized effort (with significant gestation periods) for the fruits to manifest.

Just being ***PRINCIPLED,*** having upright ***CHARACTER***, having a solid ***CONSCIENCE*** or being a soft-hearted ***HUMANITARIAN*** will not create wealth. These however do play an important role as guard-rails in the creation of **WEALTH**.

The focus of the statement of '**WEALTH** without ***WORK*** being a Sin', is more to emphasize that if a society rewards the 'lazy and undeserving' with **WEALTH**, then it would be sabotaging society's engines of wealth creation and society's own future.

Recognizing ***WORK*** as central to **WEALTH** creation, allows for the factors of production of **WEALTH** to play out to the maximum extent possible. Maximization of **WEALTH** CREATION happens when **MERITOCRACY** is placed at the core of societal endeavour.

WEALTH has a straight connect with ***WORK*** input, with ***WORK*** being the primary driver. Hence all other factors while being useful, are just supporting factors.

Conclusion

Hence, ***SACRIFICE, MORALITY, PRINCIPLE, CHARACTER, HUMANITY, CONSCIENCE*** and ***WORSHIP*** while being important, are at best secondary and supporting factors.

I will use a quote from **Rumi** to end this chapter,

"Everyone has been made
for some particular work,
and
the desire for that work
has been put in every heart."

Chapter 2

WHY CAN'T WE HAVE PLEASURE WITHOUT CONSCIENCE?

Pleasure can only lead to Happiness through the Door of One's Conscience

---

"Conscience is a man's compass."

- Vincent Van Gogh

"The first condition of happiness is a clear conscience."

- David O McKay

"Conscience is to the soul what pain is to the body. We would like to avoid pain as much as possible, but at the same time we recognize that pain is a gift from GOD. If you didn't have pain, you would destroy yourself. Pain is critical to physical preservation. And so, the conscience is critical to spiritual preservation."

- John McArthur

PLEASURE

Questions Posed

2) Why can't we have **PLEASURE** without ***CONSCIENCE***?
   a) Why can't **PLEASURE** be MORE about ***SACRIFICE*** than about ***CONSCIENCE***?
   b) Why can't **PLEASURE** be MORE about ***MORALITY*** than about ***CONSCIENCE***?
   c) Why can't **PLEASURE** be MORE about ***PRINCIPLES*** than about ***CONSCIENCE***?
   d) Why can't **PLEASURE** be MORE about ***CHARACTER*** than about **CONSCIENCE**?
   e) Why can't **PLEASURE** be MORE about ***HUMANITY*** than about ***CONSCIENCE***?

Why can't **PLEASURE** be MORE about ***WORK*** than about ***CONSCIENCE?***

a) Why can't PLEASURE be MORE about *SACRIFICE* than about *CONSCIENCE*?

PLEASURE normally stems from an act done by an individual, which makes him feel really good. Since, **PLEASURE** is more an act of taking, it has got nothing to do with ***SACRIFICE,*** which is more an act of giving.

CONSCIENCE is hence, a much better guard-rail in the act of seeking and enjoying acts, that give **PLEASURE** filled moments.

b) Why can't PLEASURE be MORE about *MORALITY* than about *CONSCIENCE*?

MORALITY is generally a broad acceptance of what is right or wrong. While ***MORALITY*** is a fair barometer, ***CONSCIENCE*** is even better as it hits one at a more individual and personal level.

The society that one was born into and grew up in, often determines what can be broadly regarded as ***MORALLY*** right or wrong in that society. Since, 'My ***MORALS*** may NOT necessarily be Your ***MORALS***', ***CONSCIENCE*** plays a stronger role to guide one in pleasure seeking activities.

Also, since, acts of **PLEASURE** are acts done for personal reasons of wanting to feel good, ***CONSCIENCE*** is a better moderator and a good primary reference.

It can also be argued that ***CONSCIENCE*** has a tighter grip on what is wrong or right in specific instances of pleasure-seeking acts, which occur at an individual level.

CONSCIENCE is a more stringent filter than just the broad-brush strokes of what constitutes ***MORALITY***.

c) Why can't PLEASURE be MORE about *PRINCIPLES* than about *CONSCIENCE*?

BOTH having a ***CONSCIENCE*** and having ***PRINCIPLES*** are important to have in one's tool kit for life. In acts of seeking happiness or **PLEASURE**, ***CONSCIENCE*** helps to self-regulate one at a more personal level. This again does NOT mean ***PRINCIPLES*** have no role, it is just that they have a secondary role.

PRINCIPLES are broadly agreed rules (related to what a grouping considers right or wrong), which are to be followed to keep to the book. Often, it relates to accepted rules in terms of that grouping. Whether that grouping is at an organizational, religious or political level.

CONSCIENCE goes beyond that, while holding one accountable to one's self, in the presence or absence of rules. Since, **PLEASURE** is experienced at an individual level, it needs to be accountable at a personal level. That personal level is one's ***CONSCIENCE***.

The ***CONSCIENCE*** can act as one's personal guide and ***GPS**, while preventing excesses and minimizing one's negative foot print arising out of the act of **PLEASURE** taking.

(***GPS** is like a '[G]uru [P]ositioning [S]ystem', as Sadhguru would have said).

d) Why can't PLEASURE be MORE about *CHARACTER* than about CONSCIENCE?

While BOTH, having a ***CONSCIENCE*** and having ***CHARACTER*** is important, in acts of seeking happiness or **PLEASURE**, ***CONSCIENCE*** regulates one at a more personal level. This again does NOT mean ***CHARACTER*** has no role, it is just that its' role is secondary.

e) Why can't PLEASURE be MORE about *HUMANITY* than about *CONSCIENCE*?

HUMANITY is a broader canvas while **PLEASURE** is derived at a personal level. Hence, ***CONSCIENCE*** (which is at an individual level) is a necessary and sufficient guide to accountability that comes with seeking **PLEASURE**.

f) Why can't PLEASURE be MORE about *WORK* than about *CONSCIENCE*?

Generally, ***WORK*** involves exerting oneself mentally and physically in a sustained effort for the purpose of generating wealth.

Hence, ***WORK*** has no standing and CANNOT be used as a guide when dealing with the domain of **PLEASURE** and ***CONSCIENCE.***

Conclusion

I will end this chapter with a MAXIM on ***CONSCIENCE***. The reader can soak into it and sleep over it as he/she imbibes it.

"There's no pillow
as soft as
a clear conscience."

- *Glen Campbell*

Chapter 3

WHY CAN'T THERE BE SCIENCE WITHOUT FACTORING HUMANITY?

Since the effect of SCIENCE is profound and can affect all of HUMANITY, concern for HUMANITY should be its' primary guiding light.

"Combine Science and Humanities."

- *Steve Jobs*

"Just as the principles of SCEINCE are Universal, Science's impact is also UNIVERSAL in SCOPE."

- *Author*

"The Sciences are the 'How' and the Humanities are the 'Why'
– Why are we here, why do we believe in the things we believe in.
I don't think you can have the 'How' without the 'Why'."

- *George Lucas*

Science

Questions Posed

3) Why can't there be **SCIENCE** without factoring ***HUMANITY***?
   a) Why can't **SCIENCE** be MORE about ***SACRIFICE*** than about ***HUMANITY***?
   b) Why can't **SCIENCE** be MORE about ***MORALITY*** than about ***HUMANITY***?
   c) Why can't **SCIENCE** be MORE about ***PRINCIPLES*** than about ***HUMANITY***?
   d) Why can't **SCIENCE** be MORE about ***CHARACTER*** than about ***HUMANITY***?
   e) Why can't **SCIENCE** be MORE about ***CONSCIENCE*** than about ***HUMANITY***?
   f) Why can't **SCIENCE** be MORE about ***WORK*** than about ***HUMANITY***?

Even on its own, **SCIENCE** is infinitely powerful. **SCIENCE** has the potential to open pathways to access the powerful forces of the Universe. While the understanding of these pathways can create paths for tremendous prosperity, it can also lead to tremendous potential destruction, if NOT guided by a concern for ***HUMANITY***.

It is important to note that as **SCIENCE** unlocks the secrets of the universe, it has an impact beyond our local communities, societies, nations and even our planet. Since, its' effect is large in scope and scale (beyond the individual, society and nations), **SCIENCE** is best guided by a concern for ***HUMANITY***.

If **SCIENCE** is divorced from its' concerns for ***HUMANITY***, it could lead to very bad outcomes. It could even cause the self-destruction of the human race. Hence, **SCIENCE** should prioritize and place ***HUMANITY*** at its' center over other factors.

a) Why can't SCIENCE be MORE about *SACRIFICE* than about *HUMANITY*?

Often, when people in positions of leadership or decision-making talk about making ***SACRIFICES***, they talk in relation to OTHERS making those sacrifice. This is often justified as being a necessity for the betterment of society, nation or ***HUMANITY***.

To understand and illustrate it, let us look at some examples:

i. Would it be right, if one did not inform the participants of a drug trial of its' potential dangers and any precautions as necessary. Can we just assume that **SCIENCE** and its' progress is more important than their safety?

ii. What if we did not take precautions (and place safeguards) before the rapid development of Artificial Intelligence because progress of science cannot be paused?

Can all these be justified on basis of progress of **SCIENCE** alone, as the ONLY thing that matters.

b) Why can't SCIENCE be MORE about *MORALITY* than about *HUMANITY*?

MORALITY is often a guidepost at a 'Individual level' or 'Societal level'. What constitutes ***MORALITY*** often varies from person to person and society to society. It can cloud judgement in terms of **SCIENCE**, whose impact is at a Universal level.

Often as children grow into adulthood, religion serves as a foundation upon which ***MORALS*** solidify. The problem is that religion often has fossilized views from a very distant past. Most religions were born multiple millennia ago. Hence, they may not have answers on how to tackle contemporary issues, such as those posed by new discoveries and inventions related to **SCIENCE.**

Example of such a Scenario:

i. Would the invention and wide acceptance of the 'Condom' be possible if ***MORALITY*** was the only consideration (in the light of certain beliefs)?

   Aren't birth control and the prevention of STDs more important than limiting beliefs for the sake of ***HUMANITY***?

ii. Would the invention and wide acceptance of the 'Vaccines' be possible if ***MORALITY*** was the only consideration (in the light of certain beliefs)?

   Isn't tackling early death of children important enough that limiting beliefs be set aside for the sake of ***HUMANITY***?

c) Why can't SCIENCE be MORE about *PRINCIPLES* than about *HUMANITY*?

When guiding decisions are to be taken at a societal level, ***PRINCIPLES*** can go beyond ***MORALs*** to serve as a good guiding post.

However as far as decisions that affect ***HUMANITY*** are concerned, just relying on ***PRINCIPLES*** alone may NOT be sufficient. It would likely fall short.

Hence, **SCIENCE** with its broad scope and scale is best addressed at the level of ***HUMANITY***. Using ***HUMANITY*** as the barometer would allow **SCIENCE** to be used to the benefit rather than, destruction of ***HUMANITY***.

d) Why can't SCIENCE be MORE about *CHARACTER* than about *HUMANITY*?

e) Why can't SCIENCE be MORE about *CONSCIENCE* than about *HUMANITY*?

While ***CHARACTER*** and ***CONSCIENCE*** are good guideposts at an 'individual level', they may NOT be suitable as a guiding post at the level of ***HUMANITY***.

Since the impact of **SCIENCE** is at a universal level, it needs a bird's eye treatment that only LOVE for ***HUMANITY*** can provide.

f) Why can't SCIENCE be MORE about *WORK* than about *HUMANITY*?

While there is no doubt that **SCIENCE** requires a large quantum of ***WORK*** as input, a decision related to the application of **SCIENCE** has to be grounded in concern for ***HUMANITY***, and not necessarily be distorted by quantum of work put in.

Conclusion

I will end this chapter with a quote on **SCIENCE** & ***HUMANITY*** by the gentleman who discovered *Pasteurization* and *Vaccines* for Rabies and Anthrax.

"Science knows no country,
because knowledge belongs to humanity, and is
the torch which illuminates the World."

- Louis Pasteur

Chapter 4

WHY CAN'T WE HAVE KNOWLEDGE WITHOUT CHARACTER?

'Knowledge is Power' and that Power in the hands of an individual can use Character as a 'Guiding hand'.

"Knowledge will give you Power, while Character (will get you) Respect."

- Bruce Lee

"Life is a reflection of Character;
Character is a reflection of Thoughts."

- Anonymous

"A person with good character can be relied upon to do 'what is right' even 'when it is difficult'."

- Author

KNOWLEDGE

Questions Posed:

4) Why should **KNOWLEDGE** be P**rimarily** about ***CHARACTER***?
   a) Why can't **KNOWLEDGE** be MORE about ***SACRIFICE*** than about ***CHARACTER***?
   b) Why can't **KNOWLEDGE** be MORE about ***MORALITY*** than about ***CHARACTER?***
   c) Why can't **KNOWLEDGE** be MORE about ***PRINCIPLES*** than about ***CHARACTER***?
   d) Why can't **KNOWLEDGE** be MORE about ***HUMANITY*** than about ***CHARACTER***?
   e) Why can't **KNOWLEDGE** be MORE about ***CONSCIENCE*** than about ***CHARAC*TER**?
   f) Why can't **KNOWLEDGE** be MORE about ***WORK*** than about ***CHARACTER***?

a) Why can't KNOWLEDGE be MORE about *SACRIFICE* than about CHARACTER?

While the pursuit and application of **KNOWLEDGE** does involve some ***SACRIFICE***, there can always be a profit motive in the pursuit of **KNOWLEDGE**.

Since, pursuit of **KNOWLEDGE** and its' application can always be fueled by a profit motive, ***SACRIFICE*** alone cannot be the cornerstone in the realm of pursuit of **KNOWLEDGE**.

b) Why can't KNOWLEDGE be MORE about *MORALITY* than about *CHARACTER?*

The 'Pursuit of **KNOWLEDGE**' is primarily, a pursuit done at an individual level. As **KNOWLEDGE** accumulates and compounds (to an individual), it puts POWER into his hands. After all, **KNOWLEDGE** is power. This power however, can be a force for good or can be sometimes misused.

The onus of how to use this **KNOWLEDGE** squarely lies on the individual. Since ***CHARACTER*** is the collection of ***MORALS*** and MENTAL qualities distinctive to an individual, the ***CHARACTER*** of the person would define as to how that knowledge gets applied.

Hence ***CHARACTER*** precedes ***MORALS***, as the power to expound the **KNOWLEDGE** gained, lies in the hands of the 'Individual'.

c) Why can't KNOWLEDGE be MORE about *PRINCIPLES* than about *CHARACTER*?

Again the 'Pursuit of **KNOWLEDGE**' is primarily by an individual. Having acquired the knowledge and knowing its' power to impact society, it is really up to the individual to decide as to how he/she would like to apply that **KNOWLEDGE.**

Since the onus is with the individual with the power in his hands at an individual level, the ***CHARACTER*** of the person would precede the ***PRINCIPLES*** in application of *that* **KNOWLEDGE.**

d) Why can't KNOWLEDGE be MORE about *HUMANITY* than about *CHARACTER*?

While ***HUMANITY*** and ***CHARACTER*** are BOTH important, the question really is why shouldn't ***HUMANITY*** be more important than ***CHARACTER*** (when it involves **KNOWLEDGE).**

HUMANITY is more about benevolence, while pursuit of **KNOWLEDGE** involves honest work. The work put in by an individual could greatly benefit society and hence, it is fair that the work be compensated fairly.

Hence, pursuit of **KNOWLEDGE** need not necessarily be completely altruistic. It can involve a profit motive while benefiting society positively.

The good ***CHARACTER*** of a person however, does play a role in making sure that the **KNOWLEDGE** is NOT misused.

Hence in pursuit of **KNOWLEDGE**, one can say ***CHARACTER*** precedes ***HUMANITY*** as a guidepost.

e) Why can't KNOWLEDGE be MORE about *CONSCIENCE* than about *CHARACTER*?

BOTH ***CHARACTER*** and ***CONSCIENCE*** operate at a more intimate and individual level. While again ***CHARACTER*** and ***CONSCIENCE*** are BOTH important, there are still nuances.

While BOTH ***CHARACTER*** and ***CONSCIENCE*** are almost interchangeable, ***CONSCIENCE*** operates more from the angle of 'TAKING', where one is at the 'RECEIVING END' experiencing it at as an individual.

The whole focus with ***CONSCIENCE*** is more on taking while leaving a minimum negative footprint. ***CONSCIENCE*** best operates in the realm of PLEASURE (which is something experienced at an individual level).

CHARACTER comes into play when one makes decisions that may involve 'taking & giving', where 'PLEASURE taking' may NOT necessarily be the central theme.

Hence, good ***CHARACTER*** is a 'necessary and sufficient' characteristic to help one navigate the responsibility of POWER that comes with the pursuit of **KNOWLEDGE** and its' application.

f) Why can't KNOWLEDGE be MORE about *WORK* than about *CHARACTER*?

WORK put in towards gaining **KNOWLEDGE** is a wonderful thing. The equation of ***WORK*** leading to **KNOWLEDGE** needs a moderator, lest the **KNOWLEDGE** becomes a ticking time bomb.

The good ***CHARACTER*** of a person can be that moderator, which helps to guide that **KNOWLEDGE** towards productive and happy outcomes for SOCIETY.

Conclusion

This chapter makes an attempt to answer the question of why ***CHARACTER*** plays a central and important role in moderating and guiding the power of the Knowledge and its' powerful and extensive applications.

Ancient Tamil poet & philosopher ***Thiruvalluvar*** expounds on the importance of carefully using knowledge for the benefit of mankind in his treatise ****Thirukkural.***

In this timeless classic ***Thirukkural,*** philosopher & poet ***Thiruvalluvar*** offers his profound wisdom when he ponders about the future of the human race he states.

"Where does the intellect lead the human race?"
He declared:
'What does humanity gain from knowledge
if
such knowledge does not make one remove
the
pain of another human being
just as
he would remove his own pain?"

***Thirukkural**

Thirukkural also popularly referred to as ***Kural*** (meaning couplets) is a compilation of **1,330 Tamil Couplets** of **7 words each**.

The ***Kurals*** or couplets cover **3 main themes** namely,

Aram (Virtue),

Porul (Wealth),

Inbam (Love).

Chapter 5

WHY CAN'T THERE BE POLITICS WITHOUT PRINCIPLES?

Why Principles are Paramount for the Smooth Conduct of Politics.

"Politics is all about consensus building in order to attain positive outcomes for society. It involves balancing 'happiness at an individual level' and 'harmony at a societal level', in a 'Live and let-Live' framework.
This can only be achieved by accommodating views from all sides, while debating them and arriving at a consensus, in a respectful and empathetic manner."

-Author

"A well laid-out manifesto which spells out the PRINCIPLES by which a political party would govern, would be a good-yard-stick to understand, what a political grouping/party promises and hopefully intends to do, if elected to govern."

-Author

POLITICS

Questions Posed:

5) Why would **POLITICS** be **PRIMARILY** about ***PRINCIPLES***?

   g) Why can't **POLITICS** be MORE about ***SACRIFICE*** than about ***PRINCIPLES***?

   h) Why can't **POLITICS** be MORE about ***MORALITY*** than about ***PRINCIPLES***?

   i) Why can't **POLITICS** be MORE about ***CHARACTER*** than about ***PRINCIPLES***?

   j) Why can't **POLITICS** be MORE about ***HUMANITY*** than about ***PRINCIPLES***?

   k) Why can't **POLITICS** be MORE about ***CONSCIENCE*** than about ***PRINCIPLES***?

   l) Why can't **POLITICS** be MORE about ***WEALTH*** than about ***PRINCIPLES***?

a) Why can't POLITICS be MORE about *SACRIFICE* than about *PRINCIPLES*?

The central objective of **POLITICS** is to create harmony, a consensus and a way forward. These have to be based on a framework of ***PRINCIPLES*** that act as a template and a guide. An approach involving ***SACRIFICE*** cannot in isolation achieve the objectives that **POLITICS** is entrusted to achieve.

As an individual it is fine for a person to enter **POLITICS** by sacrificing potential wealth, family, time or other aspects. However, on its' own ***SACRIFICE*** alone will NOT lead to positive outcomes for society.

An approach centered around governing ***PRINCIPLES*** is what should interest an electorate. A politician who lays out the ***PRINCIPLES***, and a call for action based on those principles is what an electorate would be interested in.

b) Why can't POLITICS be MORE about *MORALITY* than about *PRINCIPLES*?

To ANSWER these questions, let us try ANOTHER WAY. Let us ask MORE QUESTIONS.

- Would you disqualify someone from politics because he/she smokes?
- Would you disqualify someone from politics because he/she drinks alcohol?
- Would you disqualify someone from politics because he/she eats fast-food?
- Would you disqualify someone from politics because he/she listens to music?
- Would you disqualify someone from politics because he/she eats non-veg?
- Would you disqualify someone from politics because he/she gambles?
- Would you disqualify someone from politics because he/she is single/divorced
- Would you disqualify someone from politics because he/she has a mistress/lover?
- Would you disqualify someone from politics because he/she consumes tobacco?
- Would you disqualify someone from politics because he/she takes drugs?
- Would you disqualify someone from politics because he/she visits prostitutes?
- Would you disqualify someone from politics because he/she watches pornography?
- Would you disqualify someone from politics because of his/her sexual orientation?
- Would you disqualify someone from politics because they are illiterate?

- Would you disqualify someone from politics because of their inter-racial marriage?
- Would you disqualify someone from politics because of their inter-caste marriage?
- Would you disqualify someone from politics because they of inter-cultural marriage?
- Would you disqualify someone from politics because he/she has guns?
- Would you qualify/disqualify someone from politics because of their gender?
- Would you qualify/disqualify someone from politics because he/she is rich/poor?
- Would you qualify/disqualify someone from politics based on their race/color/caste?
- Would you qualify/disqualify someone from politics because he/she is celibate?
- Would you qualify/disqualify someone from politics based on their faith/religion?

Well, that was just a small sample, but there will always be one or more issues that one would AGREE/DISAGREE on with one another.

The questions posed above attempt to answer the question as to,

'Why personal views on ***MORALITY***', MAY NOT disqualify one to be a politician?

The reason is that **POLITICS** is about bringing to the table all, the societal views and perspectives from across the spectrum. This allows for all the views and perspectives to be heard, understood and debated, in an attempt to arrive at a consensus.

(Having said this any Politician needs to separate his personal views on ***MORALITY*** and try to work on agreed upon ***PRINCIPLES***).

It is only then, that policies can be formulated to balance 'social acceptance' with 'individual freedom'. When the balance between 'social acceptance' and 'individual freedoms' is arrived at then, harmony and happiness in society can be attained.

This would require representations across the spectrum to be represented. Therefore, politicians should be prepared to set aside their personal views on what constitutes ***MORALITY***, while embracing ***PRINCIPLEs*** agreed upon as their principal GUIDING POST.

The WORLD is a DIVERSE PLACE.

As the saying goes, 'YOUR ***MORALS*** may not be MY ***MORALS***'.

MORE importantly **POLITICS** is probably more about WHAT you 'bring to the table' and NOT JUST about your 'personal views or personal beliefs'.

Sometimes, 'Diversity of Opinion' MAY NOT be such a bad thing.

So, should the debate on ***MORALITY*** be kept out of **POLITICS**?

The question really should be, Why **POLITICS** should be more about ***PRINCIPLES***? That does NOT mean we throw away ***MORALITY.***

However, when it comes to 'POLICY MAKING' elected politicians / administrators / representatives should be able see things by setting aside their PERSONAL VIEWS or biases as what constitutes ***MORALITY***. **POLITICS** can be OPINIONATED.

It is NOT about individual OPINIONS (about what is ***MORAL*** and what is NOT), but it is about workable ***PRINCIPLES*** that one works towards for betterment of society.

PRINCIPLES of a leader/party can be on what they think society should and can agree on. These should consider the happiness and prosperity at an 'individual-level' while balancing it with harmony at a 'societal-level'.

While harmony in society can only be there if every individual is happy, the foundations for individual happiness can only happen when there is harmony in society.

BOTH are necessary and are to be in BALANCE. Also, this BALANCE does change and evolve with time. **POLITICS** needs to keep pace with changing times and aspirations of the population.

This BALANCE however, can only be achieved through debate that accommodates all view-points. It needs to be arrived at by shaping a consensus through a 'Live and let Live' approach.

WHO is ***MORALLY*** right? WHICH is a ***MORALLY*** superior view? or WHO is ***MORALLY*** wrong? as seen from an individual's standpoint, needs to be set aside as one debates with an open mind.

This is because people can and have differing views of what constitutes ***MORALITY***. Though it must be said that even a larger grouping can often agree on what constitutes ***MORALITY***. However, **POLITICS** is about hearing diverse views and debating them. Also, what constitutes ***MORALITY*** can and does change with time

So, the better approach is to start with what society can broadly WORK WITH. While Political groupings could draw out a set of ***PRINCIPLES,*** politicians need to set aside their personal biases and morals, while debating and creating new policies. This is a balancing act where the individual and societal needs, should be best met in a 'give and take' approach.

Injecting ***MORALITY*** as CENTRAL to the debate is NEVER going to lead to a solution acceptable to all. It will only complicate the debate. One would get lost in a circle of endless debates, often losing sight of what one wants to and could achieve together (by taking everyone along).

DEBATES should be anchored by ***PRINCIPLES*** without being weighed down by personal views on what is MORALLY right.

Success in **POLITICS** is ultimately about building the consensus to take society towards a more accepting, peaceful, prosperous and harmonious future.

Some ACTUAL Examples:

Would PROHIBITION of Alcohol Work?

Would Prohibition (of Alcohol) be a good idea?

In the United States, in the 1920s, prohibition was tried and it failed.

Prohibition led to bootlegging, which in turn created and nurtured criminal gangs. With criminal gangs came turf wars, and violence that spilled into the streets.

With Prohibition there was an obvious unmet demand. Gangs moved in to fill the vacuum. Interestingly, gangs like one led by famous Al Capone, had actually bought out legit businesses in the alcohol production (legit businesses had sold out when prohibition was introduced). These bought out businesses provided all the infrastructure for large scale bootlegging off the bat.

The incentive to meet demand birthed similar gangs who operated from a dark space. It did NOT eliminate the drinking of alcohol. It just pushed the trade underground.

Was alcoholism a Problem? Maybe, but is alcohol the problem (or is it alcoholism)?

So, it is complicated.

From a POLICY standpoint, would it be better to just legalize and tax the business? Would regulation be better than an outright ban. The money collected as tax, could then be used for societal messaging and in teaching kids about the danger of alcoholism. Also, it could be used to treat people who become alcoholics and help them overcome their addiction.

It would just be simplistic to ban alcohol and expect that it can be wished away. Also, many social drinkers may NOT entirely agree on an outright ban. While some may take a moral stance on the issue, others may not see it as a problem that needs an outright ban.

Regulating, taxing (calibration of taxes) and social messaging may be more acceptable and effective choices in policy making.

Also, while alcoholism for instance causes problems like drunken driving. Society may find that 'DWI' and 'OWI' laws are still inadequate to deal with the problem. 'DWI' and 'OWI' laws are still costly to enforce and do little to deter the problem.

The question is whether POLICY MAKING can be smart enough to at least partially evolve a solution, while maintaining the balance between the right of individual to drink alcohol can be balanced with the societal harmony it could disrupt.

Could the societal infringement in terms of drunken driving be tackled by SMARTER policies or legislations?

Example of a Solution to Drunken Driving:

While it may be impossible to stop a person drinking excessively and then driving on a weekend, these issues can be better tackled with some imagination.

For instance, better legislation could nudge a person visiting a bar to take a cab. One could incorporate the cost of a cab ride (to and from a bar) in the bill/check paid by the drinking patron at the bar or place of drinking. The cost could be incorporated in some way into the charges for the service at the bar.

This would allow a patron to truly enjoy his drink, without worrying about the technicalities of what could trigger a red flag in a potential breathalyzer test. While this would save a patron from potential fines and possibly serious drunken offenses, it would make the roads safer for others and lessen the load on the law enforcement.

Further, it would also free the law enforcement to pursue other serious safety issues while saving government money in enforcement.

In all, it is a win-win for the individual patron and the society as a whole. This is just one example of how one can balance the 'individual's right to happiness' with 'societal harmony'.

This is just an example of how by setting aside one's ***MORAL*** standing on an issue and understanding the issue without personal biases coloring the issue, better outcomes can be achieved.

When one is willing to set aside one's personal OPINIONS (often born out of rigid ***MORAL*** thinking) would allow for one to be able to see the OTHER person's POV (points of view) and have an 'ENABLING debate' leading to a more 'ACCEPTABLE consensus'.

POLITICS is NOT about IMPOSING one's ***MORAL*** VIEWS or OPINIONS on society. **POLITICS** is about BRINGING OUT the 'CONTRADICTING and DIVERSE VIEWS' in society and DEBATING them in a respectful and empathetic manner, thus leading to progressive policies.

POLITICS is about debate and consensus. It is a DEBATE at a SOCIETAL level, that would allow for a consensus, leading to PROGRESSIVE policy making in tune with the times. DEBATES should hence be anchored by ***PRINCIPLES*** without being weighed down by ***MORALITY.***

PRINCIPLES on the other hand are ultimately, what is good for an INCLUSIVE society. This can only be decided by accommodating views from all sides in an empathetic manner. It has to be a 'live and let live' approach. It is about attaining 'happiness at an individual level' and 'harmony at a societal level'.

This of course is NOT simple. However, most people would agree that it is more important what a POLITICIAN brings to the table in terms of ability to ACCOMMODATE diverse opinions and ability to STEER the debate towards a CONSENSUS. That is a sign of an able leader. This is best done if politicians can set aside their personal ***MORAL*** OPINIONs, to enable an EMPATHETIC and EVOLVING debate, leading to HEALTHY and INCLUSIVE outcomes.

Though this is complicated, by using ***PRINCIPLES*** (divorced from PERSONAL ***MORAL*** stand points) at the CENTRAL guidepost in politics, one would allow for the public to elect representatives for what they bring to the table, rather than their personal failing perceived or otherwise.

People in Politics should be more receptive to other's views and be more

open-minded. A non-judgmental approach with focus on solutions, rather than expounding problems, would be the better approach.

Politicians who can find solutions are generally those who are ACTIVE LISTENERs. and give a hearing to all view-points. They RESPOND with UNDERSTANDING and REASONING. This can be only done when the fog of PERSONAL ***MORALITY*** is kept aside so that, the focus can be on ***PRINCIPLES***, the diverse POVs, on the debate and driving a consensus.

PRINCIPLES on the other hand often evolve and should evolve with the times and for the 'HAPPINESS and HARMONY' of society. It balances the 'HAPPINESS and RIGHTS' at individual level with the 'HARMONY and ACCEPTANCE' at a societal level.

c) Why can't POLITICS be MORE about *CHARACTER* than about *PRINCIPLES*?

POLITICS requires an individual to have active listening, fluid thinking, ability to debate respectfully and ability to build a consensus. These are best guided by taking ***PRINCIPLES*** at the center. While no doubt a person's ***CHARACTER*** is important, it can't be the sole focus. It is necessary but NOT a sufficient characteristic in **POLITICS**.

CHARACTER is a trait at an individual level, **POLITICS** involves a group coming together to form a consensus. The focus is to be on the issue at hand and a potential solution to it. While good ***CHARACTER*** of a person is appreciated, a common minimum program can be better achieved by working with the ***PRINCIPLES*** that political groupings are willing to work on.

For instance, while at an INDIVIDUAL level, the '***CHARACTER*** of a person' is extremely important (in terms of say his INTEGRITY and HONESTY). The HONESTY only holds value in that the person would be true to the people he is serving.

The good '***CHARACTER*** of a person' can help to gauge whether the actions of a politician would be consistent with his words. However, that is NOT a proxy for a politician being able to arrive at a solution for a problem at a societal level. This is because problems are more complicated than that.

What matters are 'What are the basic ***PRINCIPLES*** a politician espouses'?

However, just honestly implementing policies guided by ineffective or impractical ***PRINCIPLES*** is NOT great for **POLITICS**. It only causes more suffering and bad outcomes.

However, willingness to listen, understand agree/disagree and form a consensus, while being guided by ***PRINCIPLES*** is a smoother and effective approach. The voting public would like to know the ***PRINCIPLES*** that the individual seeking office is articulating. His ***CHARACTER*** is thus only a supporting characteristic.

d) Why can't POLITICS be MORE about *HUMANITY* than about *PRINCIPLES*?

Most **POLITICS** is local, whether at a city, state or country level, hence focusing on local issues is more pertinent.

While ***HUMANITY*** is no less important it is just that it is a bigger objective that can only be addressed when one's own house is FIRST in order.

The practical and effective approach is to FIRST keep ***PRINCIPLES*** in view in **POLITICS.** Once this is done, the bigger goal of betterment of ***HUMANITY*** can be looked into with greater focus and efficacy.

e) Why can't POLITICS be MORE about *CONSCIENCE* than about *PRINCIPLES*?

CONSCIENCE is a guide at an individual and personal level. Often, ***CONSCIENCE*** is formed from the rights and wrongs drilled into one, as one grows up.

There is no doubt that ***CONSCIENCE*** is important in making decisions. However, **POLITICS** is a broader canvas that affects society as a whole. Right and wrong is complicated enough without introducing too many boxes to tick.

> Example:
>
> One maybe a VEGAN. It maybe against one's ***CONSCIENCE*** to hurt or kill animals.
>
> However, in such debates, one would be better off placing ***PRINCIPLES*** rather than one's personal ***CONSCIENCE*** at the center. Thereby one can have a greater chance of consensus and a way forward, rather than being stuck in an endless go-around with no resolution and way forward.

Also, one does formulate and espouse ***PRINCIPLES*** before one enters and participates in **POLITICS.** These ***PRINCIPLES*** are ultimately a ***CONSCIOUS*** act and hence using those ***PRINCIPLES*** as a guide, is in any case, an all-encompassing approach.

f) Why can't POLITICS be MORE about *WEALTH* than about *PRINCIPLES*?

POLITICS is primarily about ***SERVICE*** and NOT a vehicle to generate ***WEALTH.***

It is the business of **POLITICIANS** to create the atmosphere and the supporting policies that enable the private sector to create ***WEALTH.*** **POLITICIANS** should focus on forging a consensus and creating a harmony that would allow the citizens to do commerce and create ***WEALTH*** and prosperity.

POLITICIANS who treat **POLITICS** like a business, would do well to leave **POLITICS** and go into ***COMMERCE*** and create ***WEALTH.***

POLITICS is primarily about service. It is about helping society work through its' problems and in helping society attain harmony, while enabling commerce to progress and hum along.

Conclusion

Keeping ***PRINCIPLES*** as central to **POLITICS** would allow society to move forward and commerce to happen smoothly.

The following quote re-inforces why one should elect politicians based on ***PRINCIPLES:***

"Always vote on principle,
though you may vote alone, and
you may cherish the sweetest reflection that
your vote is never lost."

-John Quincy Adams

Chapter 6

WHY CAN'T THERE BE COMMERCE WITHOUT MORALITY?

Commerce guided by Morality can be a Powerful contributing Force for a Society to attain

---

Health, Harmony and Prosperity

"Only morality in our actions can give beauty and dignity to life."

- Albert Einstein

"It's time to place the market within a Moral framework – even if that means standing up to Companies who make life harder for parents and families."

- David Cameroon

COMMERCE

Questions Posed:

6) Why would **COMMERCE** be **PRIMARILY** about ***MORALITY***?
   a) Why can't **COMMERCE** be MORE about ***SACRIFICE*** than about ***MORALITY***?
   b) Why can't **COMMERCE** be MORE about ***PRINCIPLES*** than about ***MORALITY***?
   c) Why can't **COMMERCE** be MORE about ***CHARACTER*** than about ***MORALITY***?
   d) Why can't **COMMERCE** be MORE about ***HUMANITY*** than about ***MORALITY***?
   e) Why can't **COMMERCE** be MORE about ***CONSCIENCE*** than about ***MORALITY***?
   f) Why can't **COMMERCE** be MORE about ***WORK*** than about ***MORALITY***?

The real crux of the problem is that when we consider **COMMERCE**, it involves a profit motive. Often, decisions taken during the conduct of **COMMERCE** can be taken without oversight. Hence, ***MORALS*** often play a powerful and guiding role in **COMMERCE.** This is because the ONLY thing that stands between the 'decision maker(s)' and their 'decision(s)' is often, only the ***MORALITY*** of the decision maker(s).

Since, ***MORALS*** generally concern a BROADLY ACCEPTED distinction between right and wrong, good or bad behaviour, and the extent to which an action is right or wrong, they can serve as a good guide for the good conduct of the management of businesses.

For instance, by using ***MORALITY*** as a Compass, businesses can reduce the impact of detrimental elements like greed. Hence, when guided by our **MORALS**, we are more likely to take decisions that are more balanced and tempered.

While no decision is perfect and, while many situations often fall into grey areas, our **MORAL** Compass could guide us to navigate in **COMMERCE,** while minimizing the businesses' negative footprint.

a) Why can't COMMERCE be MORE about *SACRIFICE* than about *MORALITY*?

COMMERCE by nature involves 'Give and Take'. Decisions in business are taken with a profit motive in exchange for goods or services that common people can buy.

A 'profit motive' is central to **COMMERCE. COMMERCE** neither calls for ***PERSONAL SACRIFICE*** (which is charity) nor should it extend to ***SACRIFICING*** SOMEONE ELSE'S interests.

Our ***MORAL COMPASS*** can play a guiding role, where we don't ***SACRIFICE*** the interests of others in the pursuit of profit in **COMMERCE.** While **COMMERCE** involves a profit motive at a personal level, a good ***MORAL COMPASS*** can act as a good guide in preventing excesses.

For example:

i. Would it be OK to MAXIMISE PROFIT by overfishing at sea? Would it be OK to overfish a specie into extinction? Why, can't we just sacrifice the fish at sea for our profits?

ii. Would it be OK if we DON'T inform the participants of a drug trial of its potential dangers and precautions necessary? Can we just assume that drug development is more important and sacrifice the safety aspects of the participants?

iii. Would it be OK if a Chemical factory chooses to pollute a water source used by a nearby village, while sacrificing the health of those villagers?

iv. Would it be OK to unnecessarily Torture Animals while producing Cosmetic products?

b) Why can't COMMERCE be MORE about *PRINCIPLES* than about *MORALITY*?

While Decisions made in **COMMERCE** impact at a societal level, they are often made by management of companies in the interests of their businesses.

One can have ***CHARACTER*** and abide by ***PRINCIPLES***, but these are in the locus standi at a personal level. While a leader having ***CHARACTER*** and ***PRINCIPLES*** is great for the integrity and brand value of the business, it also needs to percolate through the ranks.

The direction a business can take often goes beyond just one individual and is based on the culture of the organization. This direction (a business takes) needs to be in congruence with the values of the organization and be in tune with the society in which it operates.

Since what is ***MORALLY*** correct can be agreed on at a broader societal level, it precedes ***CHARACTER*** (which can be flawed) or ***PRINCIPLES*** (which is a set of rules agreed to by a subset of society) while acting as a better guide.

c) Why can't COMMERCE be MORE about *CHARACTER* than about *MORALITY*?

A 'set of ***MORAL*** beliefs' distinctive to an individual constitutes ***CHARACTER***. While the formed ***CHARACTER*** of an individual is shaped by his personal morals and beliefs, ***MORALITY*** is what a society can accept at a broader level.

There is a saying 'Your ***MORALS*** need not be my ***MORALS*** which clearly illustrates that people can vary in their personal beliefs in what is ***MORALLY*** correct and what isn't. But **COMMERCE** has to base on what is more broadly agreed on as being acceptable and right. Since, **COMMERCE** through its' actions affects the broader society, ***MORALITY*** is a better guidepost.

d) Why can't COMMERCE be MORE about *HUMANITY* than about *MORALITY*?

The world of **COMMERCE** is a 'Give & Take'. **COMMERCE** provides a framework for this exchange and a framework in the creation of **WEALTH**. **COMMERCE** has been the foundation of our civilizations. It has served as the essential engine in generating wealth and progress for society.

For instance, while concerns of ***HUMANITY*** can be addressed by personal charity or by suitable allocations by the government, charity CANNOT become central to **COMMERCE.** Neither can charities operate like a business. Isn't it then best that **COMMERCE** and **CHARITY** best be kept separate and not confounded together.

Example:

Let us assume that after a decade of effort and hundreds of millions of dollars invested, a Pharma company discovers and takes to market a cure for Cancer.

Could we then tell the Pharma company to provide the drug free of charge and do so in the interest of Humanity?

Let us for instance, assume we go ahead and do so. Going forward do you think any Pharma Company in the world would bother investing and doing R&D to discover a new drug?

Wouldn't a better approach be for the Pharma company's management to price the drug to balance 'profits' with the 'pricing reach' of the drug?

In such a case, could a ***MORAL COMPASS*** be a better guide. Could it help keep greed at bay while pricing the drug? Would it help balance the interests of the Company's shareholders and employees with the public at large (with the government stepping in times of crisis or in the case of excesses)?

Basically, under normal circumstances the 'love for ***HUMANITY***' ***alone*** cannot drive drug pricing, (while relegating **COMMERCE** to the dustbin). Such an approach would be extreme socialism that would destroy the engines of **COMMERCE** (in this case the Pharma companies) and put them out of business.

Hence, mixing **COMMERCE** with altruistic intentions would complicate things and lead to poor outcomes.

e) Why can't COMMERCE be MORE about *CONSCIENCE* than about *MORALITY*?

CONSCIENCE is mushier and tougher to negotiate when set against the background of **COMMERCE.** Trying to reach a fairer and more sustainable outcome is always going to be more difficult when **COMMERCE** is added, in the 'court of ***CONSCIENCE***'.

Arguments like, 'why drugs to cure health conditions shouldn't be given for free?' (especially when one sees pictures of people suffering and dying of cancer) would constantly erode the ability to reach balanced outcomes.

In the 'court of pure ***CONSCIENCE***', the management (of the pharma company) would feel compelled to give its' products for free. However, such outcomes would destroy the very engines of **COMMERCE** and progress. It would destroy a progressive engine, that discovers new drugs. An engine that also manufactures existing drugs (at quality), making 'quality healthcare' possible.

Hence using ***MORALLITY*** as a basis and guidepost, is a much better proposition. **MORALITY** could better balance the interests of the pharma company, shareholders, employees and the prospective patients. By pricing the drug in a manner that allows for the pharma company to be profitable (and retaining the incentive to invest in further research), while balancing interests of the patient, one could attain outcomes that keep the industry sustainable and engaged in **COMMERCE**) to the benefit of all involved.

In other words, **COMMERCE** guided by ***MORALITY*** could help to contain greed, while being practical and sustainable at the same time. ***CONSCIENCE*** is mushier and more complicated. It can't serve as a primary guide for the conduct of **COMMERCE**.

f) Why can't COMMERCE be MORE about *WORK* than about *MORALITY*?

Just as in the case of a knife, (which can cut vegetables or be used to hurt someone), pure intelligence and hard-work needs a guiding hand.

A guiding hand directs the cutting edge of ***WORK*** (intelligence, hard-work and enterprise) to channelize the energies in a positive and productive direction that is beneficial to all stakeholders (including society).

While ***WORK*** is a necessary and fantastic ingredient, standalone, it could lead to poor outcomes, and sometimes even be detrimental. ***WORK*** needs a guiding hand.

In the case of **COMMERCE** where decisions are taken with a profit motive, a guiding hand in the form of ***MORALITY*** would be a good starting point.

MORALITY, which is a broader acceptable guide to actions and behaviour, would help channelize ***WORK*** in a productive direction (rather than being destructive). **COMMERCE** when guided by **MORALITY** can then direct the ***WORK*** input for the benefit of all.

Conclusion

Concluding this chapter is a quote by German Philosopher **Immanuel Kant** on the importance of ***MORALITY*** and happiness:

"Morality is not properly the doctrine of how
we may make ourselves happy,
but
how we may make ourselves worthy of happiness."

- Immanuel Kant

Chapter 7

WHY CAN'T THERE BE WORSHIP WITHOUT SACRIFICE?

When Someone is willing to SACRIFICE Something of Value (to him/her) for Something Worthier, then it can be said that the person is in WORSHIP of that Something.

"Great achievement usually born of great sacrifice,
and is never the result of selfishness."

- Napolean Hill

"People ask me about what sacrifices I've made.
I always answer:
I've made no sacrifices, I've made choices."

- Aung San Suu Kyn

"You can sacrifice and not love.
But you cannot love and not sacrifice."

- Kris Vallotton

WORSHIP

Questions Posed:

7) Why can't there be **WORSHIP** without ***SACRIFICE***?
   a) Why can't **WORSHIP** be MORE about ***MORALITY*** than about ***SACRIFICE***?
   b) Why can't **WORSHIP** be MORE about ***PRINCIPLES*** than about ***SACRIFICE***?
   c) Why can't **WORSHIP** be MORE about ***CHARACTER*** than about ***SACRIFICE***?
   d) Why can't **WORSHIP** be MORE about ***HUMANITY*** than about ***SACRIFICE***?
   e) Why can't **WORSHIP** be MORE about ***CONSCIENCE*** than about ***SACRIFICE***?
   f) Why can't **WORSHIP** be MORE about ***WORK*** than about ***SACRIFICE***?

a) Why can't WORSHIP be MORE about *MORALITY* than about *SACRIFICE*?

When one talks about ***SACRIFICE*** one is talking about giving up something at a personal level for a greater cause.

While those actions could be BOTH ***MORALLY*** right and be adorned by ***SACRIFICE***, just being ***MORALLY*** right ALONE does NOT constitute ***SACRIFICE***. Actions in any case, need to pass the test of ***MORALITY*** to be worthy.

However, to elevate actions to the heights of ***SACRIFICE***, NOT only has the cause to be worthy of **WORSHIP**, but one may also have to give-up things which one may value at individual level. In other words, be willing to ***SACRIFICE.***

Just upholding ***MORALITY*** alone, doesn't constitute **WORSHIP**. Neither is that alone, going to accomplish the higher order goals one has in mind. That would require some ***SACRIFICE*** at an individual level.

b) Why can't WORSHIP be MORE about *PRINCIPLES* than about *SACRIFICE*?

One can adore and venerate someone or a certain set of values. However, just being ***PRINCIPLED*** is NOT going to lead to a higher order action.

This is NOT to say that being ***PRINCIPLED*** is NOT important. However, just being ***PRINCIPLED*** alone ahead of willingness to give up something of value (to one), will NOT necessarily lead to higher worthy outcomes.

SACRIFICE in the act of **WORSHIP** involves giving up something of immediate value to one, in order to attain the higher purpose that one venerates.

Being ***PRINCIPLED*** is NECESSARY but NOT SUFFICIENT condition in the act of **WORSHIP**.

c) Why can't WORSHIP be MORE about *CHARACTER* than about *SACRIFICE*?

The same argument applies for ***CHARACTER***. Just having good ***CHARACTER*** is NOT going to automatically help in achieving the goals that one **WORSHIPs**.

SACRIFICE involves sometimes giving up something of value to us to attain something much worthier. One does so because one believes those goals (to be attained) are of higher value (in the order of magnitude).

Having a good ***CHARACTER*** is great and wonderful. However, to attain higher ideals, some ***SACRIFICES*** at a personal level may be necessary.

d) Why can't WORSHIP be MORE about *HUMANITY* than about *SACRIFICE*?

While this is an interesting question, love for ***HUMANITY*** standalone will not achieve the higher order outcomes.

If one **WORSHIPS** something, then one should be willing to make the personal ***SACRIFICES*** to attain those goals. While being a ***HUMANITARIAN*** is wonderful, just being a ***HUMANITARIAN*** can't be termed as **WORSHIP**.

You can love ***HUMANITY***, but unless one is willing to give up time, money and put in the effort, it does NOT elevate one's love for ***HUMANITY*** to the level of **WORSHIP**.

e) Why can't WORSHIP be MORE about *CONSCIENCE* than about *SACRIFICE*?

One can always act with one's ***CONSCIENCE*** in view. However, just being a person with ***CONSCIENCE*** and acting ***CONSCIOUSLY*** (while being a NECESSARY condition) is NOT a SUFFICIENT condition, to elevate one's action to the level of **WORSHIP**.

f) Why can't WORSHIP be MORE about *WORK* than about *SACRIFICE*?

Often, when one says ***WORK***, one is talking about effort put in with a profit motive. ***SACRIFICE*** involves giving up something that one values, in attempts to attain some higher order ideals.

WORK though can elevate itself to becoming **WORSHIP,** if one keeps it at the core of one's time, effort and focus. When one is willing to ***SACRIFICE*** and give-up one's leisure, while expending energy and focusing on one's work, then the ***WORK*** being done, could elevate itself to the stature of **WORSHIP**.

Conclusion

While **WORSHIP** is an act of devotion in a worthy cause, to elevate one's actions to the statured pedestal of **WORSHIP**, one should be willing to make ***SACRIFICES*** (whether these involve time, money or effort).

Below are a couple of quotes to give us something to think about:

"The truer measure of sacrifice isn't so much
what one gives to sacrifice
as
what one sacrifices to give."

- Elder Lynn G. Robbins

"Love is not getting, but giving.
It is sacrifice.
And sacrifice is glorious."

- Marion Milner

PART II

Administrator Read-up Essentials

Chapter 1

THE PACE OF CHANGE

Sorry, change is not going to wait and it only accelerates

"Time, tide and change wait for no one.
The only constant is change, embrace it or be left behind."

-*Author*

"Even as you think, what is imagined becomes reality."

-*Author*

In the year 2005, while I was doing my MBA, there was a group discussion taking place in class. The discussion was on technology and how it was changing the world. As each person predicted the next big thing, I proposed that tele-conferencing would be next.

As I was from India, which was a big outsourcing destination, I recognized that tele-conferencing would be a great business opportunity. Multi-nationals often had their supply chains spread around the world. This necessitated that executives spent more time on an aeroplane going from one place to another to meet people and manage their company's businesses.

As businesses at that time were going global, their executives travelled frequently to meet people who handled their supply chains, or were channel partners, customers, manufacturing partners etc. They would also travel to visit plants, manufacturing sites and other potential business partners.

In this context, to me tele-conferencing software made great sense. It would cut out unnecessary travel and save both time and money for companies. As I spoke, in distant Luxembourg City, a company that had been incorporated in 2003 was fast gaining traction.

Two visionaries *Janus Friis* from Denmark and *Niklas Zennström* from Sweden were already building such a product. The company's growth accelerated rapidly and by the year 2006 it had gained more than 100 million users who had downloaded and used the application.

The governments were so threatened by this new technology that enabled *'Voice and Video over Internet Protocol' (VVoIP)* that many of them tried to throttle, censor or regulate it. In fact, China initially banned it. Bangladesh and Oman were also against this company that had taken telecommunication to a new level. This company that had gained instant patronage by many users was *'Skype'*. 'Skype' was later acquired by *eBay* and was finally bought up by *Microsoft* in the year 2011.

Back at the classroom, I continued my discussion on telecommunication and how it would redefine the future of business and accelerate the growth of companies by facilitating a convenient platform for collaboration and enable quicker decisions that would save both money and time. While making this observation and propounding this business solution, I was completely unaware that there was this company 'Skype' that was working on 1 exactly the same problem.

I even went on to propose that since most communications were non-verbal, in the future as one engaged in discussions, one would also have 3-D holographic images of people in conference rooms. The people attending those meetings could, in reality, be seated thousands of miles away from each other in other continents.

They would, however, appear real and as if seated in the meeting being held in a given location. This would make collaboration easier and no different from the case where they would actually be physically present.

In my mind, I had imagined that just like *'Princess Leia'* who appears as a holographic image to guide *'Luke'* in early *Star Wars* movies, any employee in a company could be invoked into a meeting to discuss business matters.

At that time, it was just my imagination, but now this is a distinct reality. Now in the year 2019, after about a decade and a half after that imagination of mine, we actually have holographic images projected by holographic projectors. These actually blur the line between the real and the virtual. These images appear so real that people actually react to them as if it is truly part of their physical reality. In fact, some 3-D Holograms are so life-like it becomes impossible for our eyes to distinguish between the real and the imagined.

On a lighter note, I wish we had this kind of technology when I was in school. I would have left my virtual recorded self to attend and take notes in class, while I spent time playing soccer in the sun. Both my teacher and I would have been happy, and my teacher would think I was taking notes diligently. I presume, these are also some of the ways technologies can spread happiness!

The Pace of Technological Change

"What is a 'Pain Point' from a Customer POV (Point of View) is an 'Opportunity' from an Entrepreneur's point of view."

-Author

In the year 2016-17, I often travelled to New Delhi to meet prospective clients or investors for my start-up. In one of my visits, I stayed with my cousin in *Gurgaon*, (the place was later renamed *Gurugram*), which is a satellite township near Delhi and I caught the Metro to the city sometimes visiting Noida from thereon.

The *'Delhi Metro'* was fantastic. To save money, (bootstrapping my entrepreneurial venture and saving every rupee), I often travelled by it. It was a real boon.

Though the 'Delhi Metro' was a boon especially during summer, it did come with pain points when it came to purchasing tickets. Many patrons including yours truly had to stand and wait in a long queue to purchase tickets. Even if one bought a *'Metro card'* which could be used to access the Metro, it needed to be topped up at regular intervals.

This was bothersome, moreover, with every trip, travellers needed to find this card (women were rummaging into their handbags, men their wallets) to present it at every turnstile at both entry and exit. Here again, we would have a human traffic jam with people in queues trying to get in and get out. This irked me no doubt, but also got me thinking. From an entrepreneur's point of view, every problem was always an opportunity.

Most problems can be solved with some deep thinking done from ground up. All components in the environment should be looked at, as tools and solutions should be built with minimum complexity. This was my meditation and my passion. While there were many technologies to choose from, the ideal I then thought would be a method whereby the said amount is auto-debited from the user's e-accounts at entry and exit in accordance to the start and end of the customer's journey.

This again seemed like the best solution that could be implemented at all Metros all over India. Why, this could be applied across any means of transport. Any person with a registered account should be able to just enter and exit ANY public transportation in a city, ANYWHERE in the country without having to bother to carry cash, purchase a ticket or use a Metro card or any such system.

This could be fulfilled by reading a biometric, say an 'Iris Scan' that could be suitably placed at entry and exit points. This system would identify and charge customers to their registered accounts according to where they enter and exit the metro system. Technologies for Iris scan have long existed. Even the ability to scan a person's Iris from a greater distance had been proven possible. Hence, I began to think along those lines.

I recalled that a long time ago around June 2001, a company *'Keyhole Inc'* was incorporated and it released a very interesting software that provided the user with the ability to see high-definition images of the earth from space. It went further and had the ability to create 3-D images of objects on earth. Though it was initially used for real estate, urban planning and defence, its claim to fame and commercial success was during the 2003 invasion of Iraq.

It allowed *CNN* and its viewers to witness the war in a completely new way. It showed aerial footage of the war with 3-D views like never before. 'Keyhole Inc.' was then acquired by *Google* in the year 2004 which then integrated Keyhole's technology into its offering known as *'Google Earth'*. In the year 2004-05, I had to visit a place in Chicago. I had used 'Google

Earth' software to simulate flying over Lake Michigan into Chicago from over the Lakeshore drive side. Flying between buildings, I finally landed on the building that I had to visit. It was fun, new and exciting.

It's important to understand what goes into the creation of this technology and its building blocks. The first challenge in creating this kind of application is obtaining or having the access to high-definition images of the city from space or with aerial photography. What may be easily fulfilled by a few drones today was a lot harder in those days. In order to take a photograph from space one would need to have really sophisticated cameras. The other problem was stabilizing the camera in space which was a project in itself. However, since then, this technology has come a long way.

India had launched advanced *'CartoSat'* Satellites for remote sensing which provide for multispectral high-definition images of earth and observations from space. Ever since, India has been a world leader in imaging from space for civilian use. However, military satellites from the US and around the world are known for their incredible resolutions often being able to even read the fine print of a newspaper held by a reader sitting on a park bench. This technology has been prevalent for a very long time.

When I proposed that travellers' Iris be read from a long-distance, I imagined along the lines of this technology. As it was already in use, it only needed to be deployed in the right context to charge a customer for using public transport. By placing suitable cameras at entry and exit points this could be easily implemented.

A little more thought and I realised an Iris scan is quite intrusive and unnecessary. Facial recognition would be a better option. This was non-intrusive and more acceptable. Hence, I started working on this idea which I thought was more feasible.

I met a distinguished gentleman in early 2018 in Bengaluru. He had co-founded *'iSpirt foundation'* and was a well-wisher who I had known for over 3 to 4 years. I thought that an entrepreneur's ideas had to be tested and bounced off a third person to get more perspective. Since, this seemed to be novel and interesting I decided to discuss the idea with him.

Well, as I ran the idea past him and began to explain how facial recognition could solve long queues in public transport he smiled. He sat back and said, "Well have you heard of '*Digi-Yatra*?" I was taken aback and I shook my head and said that I had not. He said "the Indian Government in the coming months is going to unveil 'Digi-Yatra' which was a plan to incorporate facial recognition at airports to process passengers in a smooth and frictionless manner". The proposal was to enable smooth passenger movement and ease the process of entry into the airport and when boarding a flight. All this would be frictionless and at any point the traveller would not need to produce a boarding card or ticket.

The Indian government, as he had said, had already drawn up plans to invite established technological start-ups to provide services to enable such a scheme. When I looked it up, the civil aviation ministry had already mooted the idea months before.

This story just illustrates the pace at which technology is being created and adopted around the world even as we think forward. When I was an MBA student more than a decade ago and I came up with thoughts about new possibilities, it often would take decades to see them turn to reality.

Now, even the government seems to be forward thinking. If governments, which were considered old, boring, out-dated, slow, bureaucratic, unimaginative and useless, are adopting technologies and thinking ahead, then imagine what the private sector could be capable of doing.

The pace of technology and the pace of adoption and change are going to be explosively quick compared to the past. This is going to disrupt existing orders and unleash explosive 'creative destruction' which is going to change our lives and disrupt the old ways of thinking.

Every technology transforms society and the way people live. It would even bring about cultural changes. The pace and impact of technological change is increasing at an accelerating rate. Technologies have been democratized and are easily accessible. It is now cheaper to innovate and most importantly there are a young breed of entrepreneurs who believe in possibilities.

While change has always been there, the pace at which technology is catalysing the change is a new factor to contend with. It seems that truly time, tide and change wait for no one. What is imagined becomes a reality even as we think!

Chapter 2

HOW 'INFORMATION EXCHANGE' ACCELERATES THE PACE OF TECHNOLOGY AND CHANGE

Technology has the ability to feed on itself

"If I have seen further, it is by standing on the shoulders of Giants."

- Isaac Newton in 1675

"The pace of technological change and development is determined by the pace at which information is exchanged."

- Author

During the year 1996-97 in the midst of the internet boom, I was doing my M.S. in Engineering in the US and had gone to collect my assignment from one of my professors. As he handed it over to me, he pointed out at a sentence in my assignment.

It read, **"The Pace of technological change and development is determined by the pace at which information is exchanged"**. He asked me as to whose quote it was. I said it was mine. He looked at me and then smiled. He handed me the paper and I began to ponder on the sentence which I had written on the flow.

Isaac Newton had famously said that he stood on the shoulder of giants. This is not an off-hand statement. The tremendous work done by many of his predecessors, allowed Newton to go further with his theories. Of course, none of us can take complete credit for anything we do. We have only merely progressed further from what our forerunners have left unfinished.

Over centuries, the wealth of knowledge built by several civilizations was transmitted at a much slower rate than today. Information then was often carried by traders and seafarers. They travelled great distances to exchange products often bringing back not just traded commodities but also ideas and innovations.

The Arab traders not only traded with India but also carried a wealth of information and innovations back to their land and further into then Europe. Right from the concept of zero, metallurgy, astronomy, shampoo, to the refining of zinc, various other innovations had found their way from India across the globe and were carried forth by these traders.

It was never a one-way flow of information though. Cuisine from the Arab world, like *Samosas* (a baked or fried dish), the introduction of chillies and tomato from South America, *'Chinese fishing-nets'* and paper from China found their way to India.

The World and India benefitted greatly from the flow of information and ideas that were carried by these traders. However, it took hundreds of years for the exchange to happen and for the progress to accrue.

Fast forward to the 1990s, the internet was taking over the world by a storm. Access to information was at one's fingertips. This information superhighway was going to change the world. The exchange of information and consequent collaborations that were being built upon existing knowledge were going to benefit humanity in innumerable ways.

I remember when I was in high school, we used electronic typewriters to get our projects done, and boy, it was a pain. In my final year of under-graduation in 1996, we used *Word-Perfect* to get our thesis done.

While this was also painful, it was indeed a long way from typewriters that were used decades ago, when every change meant retyping the whole page again.

Using *Microsoft-Word* during my Master's thesis was such a relief. It definitely accelerated the pace at which one could complete one's work and I would often thank Bill Gates for it. Single-handedly he made it easier and quicker to do our projects, college work, and thesis. He probably saved us six months in the process!!

When the internet first came to India around 1995-96, the access was limited to a choice of text only to download or an option that included images. The government heavily controlled the internet at that time. I remember that the internet service provider was a public sector entity and that it took a really long time to connect to the internet and sometimes it didn't even happen.

A gentleman from another country was sitting by me at the internet service provider's office and was suffering the same plight. We both heard the same beep, the static and some other high-frequency sounds only familiar to internet users of that generation. It truly challenged our patience.

He then threw up his hands in exasperation and said that the government just wants to sit on everything. I concurred and said that they should let the private sector in, to allow for better and more efficient services. Well, that did not happen until much later.

When I think back about those days, I am at awe at how patient we must have been! To connect to the internet was a prolonged affair and the connection provided was a pain compared to the instant broadband or 5G connection of today.

I got access to the internet during my last year in undergrad and was trying to surf for information on universities in the US. The connection was all text, excruciatingly slow, and it often disconnected.

I remember when I first went to the United States, my mother would climb two floors to get to the computer on the top floor of our house to type out an email enquiring about how I was doing. It was the first time I had moved out of home and she was concerned.

My mother would follow set pieces of instruction to start the computer, log on to the internet and then open the email service and email me. My brother-in-law would joke that I was one of the few Indian students who had an internet savvy mother.

Over the years, as technology progressed and as it was adopted, I began to see changes in India. Companies began to use the internet to hire employees, find suppliers and get customers. From travel portals, job sites to government services, many sectors and services were beginning to have an online presence.

This saved a tremendous amount of time which would have otherwise been wasted in paperwork, finding, filing and snail mail. Technology truly accelerated the pace of work and improved productivity.

PRODUCTIVITY is a keyword. In the mid-1990s the US went through a period of accelerated growth but correspondingly lower inflation. This confounded the then chairman of the *Federal Reserve*. While it was difficult to deny that something profoundly different was happening it was clear that it was unlike all the business cycles since post-world war.

This expansion was reaching record lengths and was far stronger than expected. Growth was happening and yet inflation was subdued even in the face of tight labour markets. This completely defied logic and conventional wisdom.

Alan Greenspan, Chair of *US Federal Reserve*, did have an explanation for it. New conceptual framework and models needed to be created to understand the new phenomenon. A once in a lifetime acceleration of innovation had propelled the economy through the stratosphere. It was facilitated by computers that had vastly allowed for increased productivity. This brought about large leaps in growth without inflation.

In the words of the then Federal Reserve Chairman Alan Greenspan "The reason is that 'information innovation' lies at the root of productivity and economic growth. Its major contribution is to reduce the number of worker hours required to produce the nation's output".

To draw comparison, when my father a civil engineer by profession, needed to execute a project in the '70s, he would first have to communicate the details of the project in a typewritten paper typed in by a stenographer cum typist.

This would then be checked for errors, re-typed, inserted in to envelopes with the right address, the right number of stamps would be used and then the office assistant would reach the post office within the stipulated time and post the same to the architect's office.

The drawings were then created by hand by draughtsmen/draughtswomen who painstakingly drew every detail into chart paper on a drawing board. These drawings would then have to travel from the architect's office back to the engineer's table via snail mail to be scrutinized.

Any changes would then be communicated to the architect again using the postal service. Thus, these correspondences would continue back and forth to complete the process until the final drawing was approved. Then blueprints would be created and the final diagrams would be sent to a government approval body for an approval permit.

The government body would invariably ask for changes and this would need to be incorporated. Again, these would be communicated by snail mail to the architect's office and the drawings would need to be redone by hand. This would go on and on until the architect, engineer and the government body agree on a final diagram.

This was the process then; it would be long drawn and time consuming. These cumbersome processes and elongated timelines were required to just get the drawings ready even before construction could actually begin.

Fast forward to 2011, when I was working for a construction firm, the selection of the architect, specifications for the product and communications to the architect would be completed within a day via email.

The drawings would be made ready by the architect within 10-14 days and communicated back to us instantly, again by email. Any changes would have a turn-around of a day or two and these would be sent as an attachment to the email. This would then be sent to a government body and submitted in CDs/flash-drives. They would check for deviations in the diagram using specialised software.

Any changes and approvals thereon were done in a rapid fashion. The entire process would be compressed into a fraction of the time required otherwise. This is the power of technology, whether it is *AutoCAD*, processing software, email and now mobile devices for communication, they have all compressed the timelines for entire processes. This has given a booster shot to productivity.

Computing and communication technology have vastly accelerated the pace at which humans could make far-reaching strides and progress. In fields like biotechnology, large amounts of time were spent on setting up research and data generation rather than actual analysis.

Now, technology has freed up and enabled researchers in numerous ways. Bio-informatics and 'lab in a cloud' technologies have empowered researchers with tools to enable and accelerate their work in finding new solutions. These are just a few examples of technology as accelerated progress.

The dawn of the AI (Artificial Intelligence) is going to jumpstart the productivity of workers around the world in ways that cannot be imagined or completely grasped as of today. It is both exciting and scary what this genie in the lamp when unleased is going to do.

However, if used right we are going to see the dawn of a GOLDEN AGE of Human Civilization. However, if misused we could well end up destroying humanity and the universe going forward.

Hopefully, love, understanding, trust and compassion would be our guiding light, rather than hate, anger and mistrust. Technologies ultimately are just tools, which amplify who we choose to be. Hopefully, we choose our emotions and responses based on positive outlooks so that we survive and thrive as a human race.

The importance of Balancing
Our Collective Intelligence with Our Collective Wisdom

To put things in perspective we must however remember the words of Sir Isaac Newton who had stated that he stood on the shoulder of giants. Rome was NOT built in a day, and we owe our progress to centuries of toil of great scientists and thinkers of the past.

Today where we stand is hugely because of the struggles and sacrifices of those before us who have built the foundations of modern human civilization. While they continue to inspire us, we also need to balance our progress with wisdom from the ages, lest we end up seeding our own destruction.

Technology, science and all this progress are sharp tools that are getting sharper. They are like a sharp knife to be wielded with care and used skilfully and wisely.

The **pace of exchange of information** truly accelerates the pace at which things get done and contributes to the **accelerated pace of human progress.**

As communication technologies leapfrogged, so did the pace of exchange of information. Communication is now instantaneous and while this has had a tremendous impact on the speed at which civilisation has progressed, the pace is going into hyper drive.

If we get AI (Artificial Intelligence) right, we may be looking at warp-speeds to progress of humankind. **The faster we are able to exchange, process, analyse information, the quicker this progress is going to be.**

Advances in technology and communication are continuing to enable that!

Chapter 3

UNDERSTANDING THE BUSINESS OF BUSINESS

Educate yourself on why some businesses are more successful and enduring

---

"The key to investing is not assessing how much an industry is going to affect society,
or how much it will grow,
but rather determining the competitive advantage of any given company and, above all,
the durability of that advantage."

- Warren Buffett

"What an investor needs is the ability to correctly evaluate selected businesses. Note that word 'selected':
You don't have to be an expert on every company, or even many.
You only have to be able to evaluate companies within your circle of competence.
The size of that circle is not very important; knowing its boundaries, however, is vital"

- Warren Buffett

One of the important strategies to follow in investing is to invest in companies which are not only profitable but whose profitability is also durable. It is this durability that is the key to long term profitability.

Warren Buffett explains this concept by talking about how companies build competitive advantages by building large moats around them.

These moats are nothing but competitive advantages that prevent the invasion of competition which could quickly erode margins. Competition often leads to a price war and a race to the bottom, resulting in erosion of margins.

This would confine the businesses to a low profitability game. To look for durable profitability, it is necessary to understand the growth opportunities, competitive dynamics and business risks of the stock one considers investing in.

Competitive advantages may stem from many factors such as protected intellectual property or patents, speed and constant innovation, scale of the business which provides for entry barriers, special skill or system which could not be easily replicated, a strong hold on the market by virtue of good distribution and network, strong brand presence etc.

The **ability of a business to raise the price of its product or service without erosion of market share** is a great measure of a business's competitive advantage. This is the ultimate test of a company with sound competitive advantages.

Until 2018 (When this chapter was written), one fine example of such a company is *Apple Inc.* The company has been able to raise and maintain prices without eroding much of its market share.

This signifies a company that has so far, until the time this book was written shown great durable competitive advantages. Whether these competitive advantages, arising from a variety of factors such as strong branding and almost cult following will sustain longer has to be seen.

As of now, things seem intact despite the sad demise of its founder, the genius brand evangelist, legendary Steve Jobs.

There are differing competitive environments often tied to the structural attributes of an industry. This competitive environment can be studied by doing an industry analysis to understand which of the competitive advantages one has to take note of in that industry.

This may also change over time and one needs constant study to understand the implications of the competitive environment for corporate strategy. This is done by strategic analysis.

Porter's Five Forces

A business needs to be evaluated with strategic analysis to identify the moats it may have built around itself to ensure its competitive advantages. A good starting point would be Michael Porter's '*Five Forces*'. This is the classic starting point for **strategic analysis** to study a business's sustainability.

Porter identified the determinants of the intensity of competition in an industry. The more the intensity of competition the less attractive the business is for purchase.

Businesses in highly competitive environments do not have pricing power and tend to have products that are commoditised and marginally profitable. It is only differentiated companies with durable pricing power that will retain and remain profitable for a long time thus delivering superior return.

Porter lists the 'Five Forces' as:

1. **The Threat of Entry to the industry**
2. **The Power of Suppliers**
3. **The Power of Buyers**
4. **The Threat of Substitutes**
5. **The Rivalry among Existing Competitors**

The 'PORTER's FIVE FORCES for STRATEGY ANALYSIS and COMPETITVENESS

1. The Threat of Entry to the industry

My first experience in business was when I was 24 years of age. I had decided to open a store offering products at a discount. I was hoping that price sensitive customers would gravitate to my business and I would make up for the lack of margins with volumes.

My objective was to create a chain of discount stores much akin to a *Wal-Mart Inc.* in the making. I thought I would then have the volumes which would give me significant purchasing and bargaining power when I bought my wares from my suppliers and manufacturers.

This would provide an adequate price cushion to sell at unbeatable prices. This in turn would further my competitive advantage which none would be able to match. 'Good strategy' you may say. Well, I thought so too. I had thought that I needed to get past the first store, create a working model that was profitable as a unit and raise money for expansion. Also, I needed to do all this quickly.

I went on to start my business, but as luck would have it, within a span of two months, three other businesses opened stores based on the same concept in nearby locations. The market was not big enough for the four of us. We were in a race to the bottom.

I took a tough call and bailed out early, saving myself from damaging losses. The three other businesses slugged it out and finally closed one after the other with massive losses.

I chose to narrate this example, to illustrate how businesses fail to be competitive on the long term, especially when there are very few barriers to entry. They would have to face severe competition where 'price' is the only differentiator.

This would lead to price wars and limited profitability, if any.

Hence, the threat to entry into a business is a threat that diminishes a company's competitive advantage and pricing power.

Often, in such a scenario you have to be a 'price taker' as they say in economics rather than a 'price leader'. This in turn means lower margins and inability to increase price without losing market share.

Unless, one had competitive advantages such as significant scale (volumes) and hence ability to bargain with suppliers, it would leave one non-differentiated and vulnerable to competition.

The only way to win in such a scenario is to have deep pockets, haemorrhage your competition and be among the last few men standing. In this manner, one could create an oligopoly and be able to dictate price with fewer competitors clamouring for market share.

Another example, of a business with low entry barriers is the restaurant business. Anyone with some capital and a little homework could open a restaurant. We all would have seen a number of restaurants that have opened and shut shop within a short span of time.

To be successful, a restaurant would need to build customer loyalty and would need to be situated in the right location, such as a busy business district. This is not an easy task because starting a restaurant is a business anyone could get into and yet staying in the business is challenging as it faces intense competition for the same set of customers.

On the flip side businesses such as *VISA* and *MasterCard* have been durable businesses despite the intensive efforts to dislodge them. While they would face significant threats in the future because of changes in technology and consumer behaviour, for the moment they have significant competitive advantages.

They have established a massive data processing network, huge customer base, tied up with banks and enrolled merchants. It would take a lot to dislodge them in the markets they operate and dominate. A new incumbent would have a chicken and egg problem and would be caught between finding new customers and enrolling merchants.

High entry barriers can take on many forms, such as high capital investment as in aerospace, large distribution network (as in companies such as the car manufacturer Maruthi Suzuki in INDIA), patent protection as in the pharmaceutical industries, or regulation as in utilities.

2. The Power of Suppliers

Suppliers may be able to raise prices or even restrict the supply of raw materials and key inputs necessary for a company. A good example is a highly unionized company, where workers or the suppliers of labour may wield huge powers when compared to a non-unionized company. An example is General Motors in the US. Here the UAW or the Union for Auto Workers wields significant power and is therefore able to negotiate better pay.

However, in the process this has limited the competitiveness of *General Motors*. The manufacturing of cars in Mexico makes *General Motors* a more profitable company. For years, the Unions have resisted the migration of their jobs to Mexico.

Similarly, a supplier of scarce or limited parts may possess significant pricing power while negotiating with a purchasing company. Hence, the suppliers of key inputs and their negotiation power with the core company affect the core company's competitiveness.

Andrew Carnegie the self-made steel tycoon and one of the richest men to have ever lived, built his steel empire and adopted vertical backward integration of his business by buying up mines and the railroads that ferry the coal and iron ore to his plants.

In this manner, he avoided the problems of input price fluctuations, nullified the power of suppliers and maintained his company's competitiveness. However, during the course of building his empire, he had to tackle the problems he faced with the labour unions.

3. The Power of Buyers

Often large automobile companies buy from smaller auto part makers. Hence as they are the largest buyers, they enjoy the advantage of setting the price of auto parts sold to them. This allows these large automobile companies to be tough negotiators. Often, by virtue of being the sole buyers they become price setters. By doing so, depending on the position of the sellers, these buyers would exercise their power of being the end customer for these suppliers and bully them into lowering prices. In this process auto companies would increase their competitiveness while auto part makers would have to do with limits on their profit margins.

Another example of the power of buyers is in the airline industry. Despite being in a glamorous business, having entry barriers and being a business which is capital intensive, not many airlines around the world have been greatly profitable. Nowadays, consumers have great power.

The power of the internet and power of instant information that is easily accessible allows these customers to choose the lowest ticketing prices, thus forcing airline companies to price their offerings competitively. This keeps airline margins and the business under constant pressure affecting the profitability of the players in the airline industry.

4. The Threat of Substitutes

Even established brands and businesses suffer as close substitutes erode their sales, margins and brand. For example, during times of recession customers may buy cheaper beer by trading down from premium brands. When low-priced brands are substitutes for premium brands in the face of restricted budgets, it affects the ability of premium brands to increase price. Hence brands would lose their pricing power.

'*Rotomac*' a popular pen brand in India was one such company that was destroyed by cheaper substitutes. *Rotomac* was a relatively premium brand in its mid segment. However, its margins and sales were severely eroded with the arrival of cheaper pens which were sold in large numbers.

This destroyed *Rotomac's* market share and squeezed its margins. Unfortunately, as of early 2018, as its sales slipped further the company went into major losses and even got embroiled in a scam.

Over time, disruptive technologies could increase 'substitution risk'. With the invention of the aeroplane, travel by steamships almost disappeared. Newspapers which were considered a pretty steady business were rocked by television and then the internet. The television and the internet became substitutes for the manner of delivery of news and information.

Similarly, recorded music shifted from records to tapes to compact disks to Mp3 and other forms of digital media such as streaming. These are all examples of how the landscape of any business could change with the tides of new technologies, better or cheaper substitutes.

Another example is how the 'call-centre' or 'customer-support' business could be disrupted by AI (Artificial intelligence). There is an imminent possibility of these businesses being replaced by 'Auto-bots' which understand and answer customer queries with minimal intervention or supervision.

5. The Rivalry among Existing Competitors

This factor is a function of the industry's competitive structure. Fragmented industries whose markets are divided among smaller competitors, have high fixed costs, high exit costs and products that are not differentiated (commoditized), often face intense rivalry. Companies in a more competitive landscape have less cash flow predictability and have higher credit risk than companies in a less competitive landscape.

An example of high fixed costs playing truant is the computer memory market. Even though the market is highly concentrated with only four players controlling 75% of the market, the market is highly competitive. Since one DRAM chip is similar to another and because of the high capital investment involved to establish a manufacturing unit, the players have huge incentive to capture market share.

There are large economies of scale involved and capturing market share by keeping prices lower means, that the industry is not wildly profitable as you may expect. This is another example where rivalry among competitors keeps the prices under check. While all forces are important, the first and fifth are of particular interest and wield big influence on whether a company in an industry is competitive or not.

Important Questions to Ask while Evaluating a Company for Competitiveness

Some of the important questions one needs to analyse while evaluating a company for investments include:

- *What are the barriers to entry?*
- *Is it difficult or easy for a new competitor to challenge incumbents? Relatively low entry barriers imply that the threat of new entrants is relatively high.*

- *How concentrated is the industry? Do smaller number of companies control the market or does the market have relatively large number of players; each with a small market share?*
- *What are the capacity levels? Based on existing investment, how much of the goods or services can be delivered in a given time frame?*
- *Is there chronic over- or under-capacity, or do supply and demand tend to come into balance reasonably quickly in the industry?*
- *How stable are market shares? Is there a constant fluctuation in market share of companies?*
- *Where is the industry in its life cycle? Are there meaningful growth prospects, or is demand stagnating or declining?*
- *How important is price to the customer in his purchasing decision?*

It is important to analyse all these questions while making a long-term investment. Before investing in the stocks of a company, one must evaluate how durable the company's competitive advantage is within the sector under consideration.

Other Factors that affect Competitiveness

The other factors that affect industry competitiveness include:

- Industry concentration:

  Often, if an industry is highly fragmented, it is highly competitive and its' pricing power is limited.

  However, even if an industry is concentrated, it is not necessarily a sign that pricing power exists in the industry and there is rational competition.

- The Effect of Production Capacity:

  The tighter the production capacity, the greater the pricing power for the participants in an industry.

  Overcapacity kills pricing power making the participants more desperate to sell, which causes a loss in pricing power.

While considering this factor one must also consider future capacity and how long it would take for the supply and demand to come into equilibrium.

- The Effect of Market Stability:

  Stable market share often indicates less competitive industries with good pricing power. In highly competitive spaces there is limitation on pricing power.

- An Industry's position in the Life Cycle:

The five stages of an industry's life cycle according to the 'Hill and Jones' model are:

- Embryonic
- Growth
- Shakeout
- Mature
- Decline

Since companies and industries tend to evolve over time, as they go through these cycles, they usually experience significant changes in both their growth rate and profitability. Hence the stage of the industry has to be closely monitored.

'Sunset' industries in **decline stage** face possible decline and may redeploy capital if unsustainable. Companies in the **shakeout stage** on the other hand face the squeeze as competition intensifies and they could merge or be eliminated in favour of more efficient companies.

Companies in the **growth stage** face the least pricing and competitive pressures. However, they are under pressure to increase their market share and capture as much of the market as possible before there is a shakeout.

Companies in the **embryonic stage** are looking to increase awareness of their product, generate visibility and develop distribution channels.

Hence, the competitive landscape for different industries is different and is based on the stage of life cycle in play.

- Price Competition and Customer Thinking:

  The customer is king, and often the minute and subtle preferences of the customer significantly affect the way the businesses would compete. Whatever influences the customer's purchasing decisions is going to be the focus of the competitive rivalry in the industry and is hence very important. Normally if price is a major factor that affects the customer's purchasing decisions, then the industry would be very competitive.

A good example of this is the airline industry. The customer always compares prices on the internet while purchasing a ticket. This makes the industry extremely price sensitive and price conscious.

Price is a major factor affecting customer purchase decisions and hence the airline industry as a whole is focused on price and is very competitive.

Other factors that affect industry growth, risk and profitability are:

a. Technology:

   Technology can play a disruptive role in making or breaking businesses. The coming of the internet saw the arrival of companies such as *Amazon* and *Alibaba*, which have pretty much taken over the e-commerce market in US and China respectively. Spending has shifted and transactions have moved from offline, retail stores to online e-commerce portals. Interestingly Alibaba is pioneering an 'Online cum Offline' retail model in China. This is being replicated by the major players in the Indian market.

b. Demographics:

   As the majority of young India enters the work force, the demand for goods and services in the first half of this century is expected to skyrocket in INDIA. The new found purchasing power and consequent rise in demand are examples of the demographic dividend playing out. Similarly, in the US while the Baby Boomer generation grows old, businesses in the health care segment and health care services are expected to prosper and make substantial gains.

c. Government:

   Government regulations, rules and laws have the ability to alter the landscape of businesses. The deregulation of the telecommunication industry saw the break-up of AT&T in the US. In INDIA, the deregulation of the banking sector saw the rise of privately held banks such as ICICI, Axis and HDFC. Also, in India the deregulation of television lead to the establishment of the humungous number of private channels both for entertainment and news broadcast.

d. Social factors:

   Social trends, fashions, slowly seep into the mainstream changing the way businesses run. Again, it can be seen in INDIA that as the demographic dividend is playing out; casual dining and eating out have begun to take hold while grocery delivery and food delivery apps have proliferated.

Around the world hailing a cab has undergone a revolution with UBER and OLA in INDIA. All these changes are because of the changes in consumer behaviour and because society is changing the way it engages with businesses.

PORTER'S 'THREE Competitive Strategies'

It is Imperative to understand how a company would respond to threats and opportunities presented by the external environment. The analyst while analysing the strategy of the company should look into whether the strategy of the company is primarily defensive or offensive. The research should also examine how the company seeks to go about implementing such a strategy.

Porter has identified THREE chief competitive strategies

- **COST LEADERSHIP STRATEGY**
- **DIFFERENTIATION STRATEGY**
- **FOCUS STRATEGY**

COST LEADERSHIP STRATEGY

In a 'LOW-COST STRATEGY' the company aims to become the low-cost leader producer. By gaining maximum market share the company would still be able to turn a decent profit. It is a volumes game.

In case of intense rivalry, the pricing may even become predatory, and could be aimed at driving the competition out of business.

This is sometimes achieved with a loss in near term profitability. The objective of the strategy is to oust the competition with price and gain dominant market share. Later, with a dominant market hold, the company would increase prices to recoup any lost opportunities.

A classic example of this is the mobile network operations business in INDIA. The entry of Mukesh Ambani's *'Jio'* pretty much shook up the market with a very aggressive campaign offering six months of free data and voice. *'Jio'* then went on to completely stun the market with aggressive pricing forcing out many established players and causing the merger or buyout of smaller players. It completely took the market by storm with a 'Cost leadership' strategy as its central theme.

Companies following a low-cost strategy must have tight control over costs, efficient operations, efficient reporting systems, proper incentives for managers to motivate them and deep pockets with patient investors to tide over the initial difficult times. They may have to invest in productivity improving capital equipment and finance the investment with low capital costs.

DIFFERENTIATION STRATEGY

In a 'DIFFERENTIATION STRATEGY' the company hopes to establish unique products/services that are unique in quality, type or means of distribution. To be successful the pricing of the product must cover their differentiation and must appeal to the end consumer to be sustainable over time.

Often, companies that pursue this strategy must have strong market research and must invest in other industry specific research and development. They would also need to constantly differentiate their products and would need to identify new products/services which their customers would accept and love.

The customer would need to pay that extra for the product and this would happen only if the customers love the product. Such a strategy involves employing creative and inventive people. It is an expensive and premium strategy with massive benefits.

Apple's iPhone is a product that is constantly upgraded with new features to differentiate it from the competition. Apple is able to charge a premium for its products because the products are differentiated and the customers swear by it.

The love of the customers and the lack of immediate comparable mobile phones in the market, translates into big dollars for Apple.

FOCUS STRATEGY

The 'FOCUS STRATEGY' involves seeking a competitive advantage within a target segment or segment of an industry. Any niche focus segment that would have potential demand would do well, for example children's clothing.

A number of companies have come about in INDIA that exclusively cater to the needs of new parents and their new-born children and toddlers.

This is an example of a 'Focus' strategy, where instead of focusing on the clothing and garments for the whole population one focuses only on one segment.

'Fabindia' is a niche chain of garments stores in India that retails ethnic wear, hand woven garments and eco-friendly garments with vegetable dyes. It began early, has been one of the pioneers in this differentiated 'focus' segment and has thus carved a niche for itself.

The brand has now become synonymous with ethnic wear and has a fan following among the elite and foreigners alike.

Such a strategy of focusing on profitable segments on the marketplace is an example of the 'Focus' strategy.

CONCLUSION

To value a company, it is important to know where it stands in the competitive landscape. We need to know whether its advantages are enduring and whether it has durable pricing to pull through the ravages of time.

This is the reason why it is necessary to analyse the industry, the landscape and the potential threats and opportunities through the prism of the discussions in this chapter. The factors discussed here are pointers to the competitiveness and profitability of a company.

Before making concentrated bets, it is best to be in the know about how the company fares against the backdrop of these pointers. Hence, this chapter is particularly important to assess the enduring profitability and value of a company.

Chapter 4

'CREATIVE DESTRUCTION' AT ITS BEST

Creative destruction is the upheaval that technology would un-lease in the job market 'destroying' and 'creating' a new wave of jobs and new verticals

---

"The best way to drive your future is to be in the driver's seat and create it."

- *Author*

"Change is the only constant, it comes in waves like the waves in an ocean, the best way to deal with it is to surf it, not fight it."

- *Author*

In the year 1977, the Tatas of India proposed to the government the complete computerisation of the tax administration system.

This was rejected by the then finance minister of India, Charan Singh, and India missed a golden opportunity to implement a fully computerised tax administration system way back in the late '70s.

This is chronicled in a book by management strategist Shashank Shah in his book titled 'The Tata Group: From Torchbearers to Trailblazers'. The book was released on November 29, 2018, to coincide with the completion of 150 years of The Tata Group and the death anniversary of JRD Tata.

In 1977, the then Prime Minister of India, Ms. Indira Gandhi, and her government had rejected computerisation and reasoned that introduction of computers would lead to the loss of jobs and cause mass unemployment.

It is ironic that years later, the introduction of computers and creation of the software industry created more high paying jobs and swelled the middle class of this vast country than any other sector. This just goes to show how simplistic straight-line thinking cannot visualise the future.

While advancement in technology over the last century has caused a quantum jump in productivity, it has caused the creative destruction of the job market. This in turn left many of those people who did not upgrade their skill, stranded in the job market. Yet it did provide great opportunity to people who adapted to the change and learnt new skills. These people thrived with the change.

These changes have caused groups of people to be left behind, but it did create a path to riches for those others who were willing to adapt. These vagaries have sometimes been responsible for transformation of society.

They have also caused political upheaval, as witnessed by the unexpected election of Mr. Donald Trump as the 45th President of the United States.

Trump was powered by disaffected voters who were unhappy with the job losses and lack of opportunity in what is called the "rust belt" of the United States of America. This is where the manufacturing jobs that once held roost disappeared.

These narrations go to show the complex dynamics of how technology impacts society and how changes cannot be easily foretold. The future could unravel many dimensions. Often, the unravelling may not be in the manner that people may have expected it to be.

Job Losses

Society has a love-hate relationship with technology. People usually do not embrace or adapt to changes in technology, as any change causes a shift in the current equilibrium, which requires them to get out of their comfort zone.

Any shift that may affect the stability of their lives and society in general is not welcome, as all are happy in their state of inertia. If technology needs to be adopted it needs to be compelling.

There are always places in the world where fear of job losses and possibility of unintended consequences can cause governments to slow or forestall the adoption of new technology.

Examples of these abound. The greatest challenge faced by companies that create new technologies is in bringing about a behavioural change and roping in early adopters who are willing to adapt and try these innovations.

Some companies and their products/services are so compelling that they achieve this more easily than the others. One of the most successful start-ups of our times, Uber, is one such example. It was ultimately a game changer. The business model and mobile app were widely well received. The market then was made up of taxi operators who owned a fleet of taxis or many individual taxi drivers operating from a variety of stands.

Uber thrived as the taxi drivers did not have to scout for passengers and the consumers had embraced the convenience of hailing the cabs for hire on their mobile phones.

The local governments then intervened and brought in regulations and protectionist policies. These spokes that were brought in attempted to hinder the smooth functioning of the new entity, and to protect and maintain the old guard.

Slowly however, those who were capable of change embraced it, while the others retired or changed their working style and ways of doing business. These are examples of how friction is caused by new entrants and how stakeholders in the mix adapt or stall.

While some gain advantage and some are disadvantaged. Change remains the only constant as creative destruction unfolds. The most feared change that comes with new technology and with creative destruction is job losses.

There was a time before computers, in the '50s, '60s and '70s of the last century, when the knowledge of 'short hand' (an abbreviated symbolic writing method used by secretaries to jot notes and write down minutes of meetings) and 'typing' were highly valued skills. Those skilled in them fetched high paying jobs.

There was a time when a large number of people with typing and short-hand skills headed to Mumbai via trains from many other parts of India. The trains were popular and were nicknamed 'Typist Gadis' or train carriages that carried typists. Being a stenographer was a sought-after skill and companies headquartered in Mumbai offered great opportunities for people with such skill sets.

Nowadays, with the winds change, short-hand and stenography are dying skills that are both unnecessary and obsolete. Stenographers are a dying breed. Technology has progressed to such an extent that even 'personal secretaries' who were themselves a dwindling breed, would soon be replaced by 'personal assistants' programmes.

These would be programmes that run on AI (Artificial intelligence) and do everything from scheduling and booking itinerary to finding one a cab. While these changes have improved productivity, they have eliminated and will eliminate low level jobs in the future. These will cause disruptions that will impact society.

India in the first two decades of this century, rode the wave of outsourced software services, *BPOs (Business Process Outsourcing), KPOs (Knowledge Process Outsourcing)* and the low skilled call centre services. These created millions of jobs for the masses in India but also as technology progresses in leaps and bounds, these very jobs could see a decline in the future. The low-level functions in these jobs could soon be automated and replaced.

As India has been moving up the value chain, we have seen the migration of call centre jobs to countries such as Philippines. New technologies in the horizon would soon cause new kinds of disruptions in the job market for call centre employees.

'Chat bots' and programs that mimic call-centre executives driven by AI (Artificial Intelligence) would soon replace majority of the jobs in the call centre industry. These would not only cut costs for companies in their customer service operations, but result in job losses starting at the lowest levels of call-centre operations.

It is not just call-centre employees who would be affected, but software professionals whose jobs could be automated, would also find themselves facing job losses as companies automate mid-managerial level jobs to bring in cost efficiencies and shrink payrolls.

While software outsourcing companies are set to see increase in profitability as they eliminate payroll, many jobs in this industry would become redundant. New skills and fresh hands would replace those with old skills and jaded experience. These job losses are not just confined to developing countries but developed countries will also face their own set of challenges.

Changes in the Developed World

While one may be lulled into thinking that job losses would only occur in developing countries, this thought is far from the truth. In the developed world, while blue collar jobs were the early casualties of outsourced manufacturing which caused extreme job losses, people often believed that jobs such as truck driving could not be outsourced and were secure. There are an estimated 3.5 million professional truck drivers in the United States of America.

Annually, all these drivers combined drive about 400 billion miles and haul more than 10 billion tons of freight. The truth is that while blue collar jobs in manufacturing did get outsourced, they also got automated as machines began to take over the load of manufacturing. During this entire period, people who were truck drivers or cab drivers (though they performed by the lowest rungs in industrialised societies) had secure jobs.

Now, it is believed that by the year 2025 we are going to see a revolution with driverless cars/trucks and drone delivery mechanisms which are going to begin to eliminate jobs for people who are truck drivers, cab drivers and delivery boys. Jobs that were once thought to be safe in the developed world are going to be made redundant by technology and would be under threat.

Low level jobs including those created by companies like Uber would also come under threat. It is estimated that there are over a quarter million taxi drivers in the US and at any point of time, there are more than three quarter million drivers that are driving for Uber alone. In the future, the number of jobs in the trucking and travel industry will shrink or be eliminated.

Even e-commerce and food delivery businesses would be impacted if drone deliveries come into vogue. The only thing that stops drone deliveries from being main stream is really a regulatory nod. Once the skies are opened for drone deliveries and proper collision prevention and sky regulation mechanisms are evolved, it would cease to be some science fiction and turn into reality. It would be happening in the skies above us as we go about our day-today work.

Change on an Industrial Scale

With solar power, electric vehicles, autonomous vehicles, and transport for hire coming of age, we are going to see tectonic shifts in the industry. This is going to create and destroy jobs on an unprecedented scale.

Large industries as we know it are going to disappear and new larger ones are going to appear. New skill sets are going to be required, while older skill sets would be redundant and useless.

Insurance Industry

The Insurance industry is going to see the disappearance of entire verticals. Car insurance is going to be the first casualty.

With AVs 'Autonomous Vehicles' becoming the norm we are going to see a drastic fall in accident and accident claims, making the car insurance industry shrink and potentially even disappear.

Oil and Coal Industry

With the coming of EVs (Electric Vehicles) the entire oil industrial behemoth is going to totter towards extinction. The growth of alternative energy sources such as solar power is going to accelerate this demise.

These technologies are becoming economically viable and within a couple of decades, (to be charitable with time), we are going to see the death of the oil and coal industries.

The epitaph of the coal industry is going to be written as the solar power technologies begin to eclipse the viability of coal as a power source. The oil industry is going to crash and burn with the EVs shooting down this high-flying industry that has powered the modern era. We will soon witness the death of the 'carbon economy' as we know it.

Car Industry

We may see new players emerging in the automotive industry with EVs and automated vehicles taking over. Unless, the entrenched players make a change they may become extinct.

Further, we may notice that fewer cars would be needed as the utilization factor of cars goes up with shared services such as *Uber*. Also, with the coming of EVs (Electric Vehicles) which undergo little wear and tear, people would not be looking to replace their cars ever so often.

Potentially we may also see Green Hydrogen or Green Methanol powered vehicles. These would leave very small footprint on the environment and be able to match the current ICE [Internal Combustion Engines] in their performance and cost metrics.

Further Depths to which Technology can Create Change

For long it was also believed that only routine jobs like factory jobs which were based on a set of rules or tasks could be automated or computerized. Now, with advancement in technologies it has dawned on the public that even jobs that required personnel in a less predictable environment such as driving cars could face the heat of technological change.

However, it was always assumed that professions that were wrapped in semantics and language could never be computerized. Well, that is also about to change with advances in artificial intelligence and technology. The routine task of sifting through documents and looking for specific information or relevant paragraphs has become redundant.

This has begun to make an impact on a number of professions that were considered safe from both outsourcing and automation. Though these changes would begin to change the way things are done over next few years, the lull before the storm is being endured with bated breath.

Impact on the Legal Profession

Many young Americans have nurtured their dreams of becoming lawyers and ultimately rising to the top as partner in a law firm.

Fed on a steady diet of onscreen action and drama of legal professionals, right from *'L.A. Law'*, *'Law & Order'*, *'The Practice'*, *'Boston Legal'* to later shows such as *'The Good Wife'* and *'Suits'*, the glamour of life in the legal profession has drawn many youngsters to pick up law as their profession of choice.

Many flocked to law school taking hundreds of thousands of dollars in educational loans with the hope of a great life. The dream seemed all set, until...

Enter Watson, no not the one in *'Sherlock Holmes'*, this one is by IBM. Named after the first CEO of IBM, Thomas J. Watson, Watson is a super computer that processes at the phenomenal rate of 80 teraflops per second that is 80 trillion floating points per second.

It can process 500 Gigabytes or an equivalent of a million books per second. It can replicate the ability of a high-level human brain to answer questions. It has access to servers that have a combined storage of hundreds of millions of pages and processes information taking into consideration over six million logical rules.

Well, now you may think this is a big machine that is bigger than a Space Shuttle. Sorry to blow your bubble, all it needs is a space as small as a room that can accommodate a dozen refrigerators!

In recent times the space required to house IBM Watson as a cloud delivered, enterprise ready solution has shrunk further and it can be accommodated in a space as small as three stacked pizza boxes. Moreover, its performance is said to have improved 23 times over.

When *'Deep Blue'*, the AI machine from IBM defeated Garry Kasparov in 1997, the true power of harnessing 'Artificial intelligence' had begun to catch the attention and imagination of the public.

This got the IBM researchers thinking and led to the creation of *IBM's 'Watson'*. The computer system was initially developed for the quiz show *'Jeopardy'*. It went on to compete and in 2011, it won against legendary champions of the show to win the first place and $1 million cash prize.

Application of Watson's cognitive computing ability has vast applications. Right from law to medicine, the field is entirely open. Operations on huge volumes of unstructured data are possible and are backed by complex analytics and deep mining abilities.

In the month of May of the year 2016, an Ohio based firm called *BakerHosteler* signed up for a legal 'expert system' based on the abilities of this super computer. That system had the ability to mine data from about a billion text documents, analyse the contents and provide pin point answers to complex questions in a jiffy.

Combined with Natural Language Processing it could respond to questions related to law by translating any legal documents in normal spoken or written English language.

With IBM Watson gradually taking over the lawyer's profession and with its ability to deliver results with over 90% accuracy compared to just 70% for humans, it may not be long before the payrolls at law firms shrink.

Freshly minted young American graduates in law are not getting jobs because with IBM Watson one could get legal advice within seconds from anywhere, at any place and at any time.

With these possibilities, in the future, entry level legal advice would be available for cheap and would be available on call. There would be less need for entry level lawyers in law firms. It is estimated that any research or due diligence can be entirely done by such a system and a study report suggests that this would reduce the need of entry level lawyers by 24%.

Impact on the Field of Medicine

IBM Watson is also set to revolutionise medicine. It is being used in the field of Oncology to detect Cancer and in many instances, they have found it to be more accurate than doctors and nurses. In the year 2016, *Manipal Hospitals* of India, launched IBM Watson for cancer patients to be guided to pick cancer care options.

In fact, Manipal Hospitals offers this technology to patients online through their website and is the first in the world to do so. All these changes herald a new beginning in the field of medicine.

Though there are numerous challenges in the ultimate delivery of results, this could completely overhaul the system. The die for change has been cast and it is only a matter of time before technologies would start providing answers.

IBM Watson has wide applications right from financial service industry, education, weather forecasting, to water conservation. The future would be vastly different once IBM Watson and its successors/competitors come through with their complete potential suite of applications. Well, is this just the lull before the storm?

Creative Destruction

"Remember today is the tomorrow you worried about yesterday."

- *Dale Carnegie*

"But there is always creative destruction in markets:
There are always new winners taking the place of those that are.
So, if you look at the market's surface it may appear flat, but there's always huge turbulence taking place within."

- *Kerr Neilson*

'Creative destruction' is a given and is essential and important for the progress of mankind. Technology, the economy and the job market will always be in a state of flux.

The only questions that remains are "Are you aware of it?" and "Are you prepared for it?" There is nothing that is going to stop the creation and destruction of industries and maybe entire verticals.

'Fluid thinking' and 'agile adaptations' are the essential attributes for survival and success of individuals in this new future.

Those who are cushy in their comfort zones and those who cling on to the past and have fixed ways of doing things are going to find themselves left behind as sweeping changes bring about the need to adapt to the changing shape of the future.

Those who do adapt will thrive, while the rest will be left with nothing but nostalgia!

Chapter 5

FACTORS THAT ARE RESPONSIBLE FOR HIGH REAL ESTATE PRICES IN INDIA

Understanding the factors behind High Real Estate Prices

"Land monopoly is not only monopoly, but it is by far the greatest of monopolies; it is a perpetual monopoly, and it is the mother of all other forms of monopoly."

- *Winston Churchill*

"I would give a thousand furlongs of sea for an acre of barren ground."

- *William Shakespeare*

In this chapter we shall discuss the obvious and non-obvious factors affecting real estate prices. Many of these factors interact with other market factors differently and cause varied effects. We shall try to list as many as possible.

EFFECTIVE DEMAND

Affordability and Price

My father often says if one has a lot of gold and then tries selling it in an isolated impoverished village chances are that one may not get much for it. This analogy was of course in the context of the widening gap between affordability of the masses and the prices of real estate. He means to say, 'what is the point of the market quoting higher and higher prices for real estate, when the affordability is not keeping pace?'

There are two aspects to this; the first being valuation versus real estate price. (The book 'THE REAL DEAL' is a recommended read if one wanted to dive deeper into the subject of 'Price Vs Valuation' in the real estate field).

The second aspect which is the primary point I am trying to stress on, is about price and "effective demand." Price is not only something that a consumer is 'willing to pay', but also what he **CAN** pay, in other words 'affordability'. Despite gold being perceived valuable, if the impoverished villagers cannot afford to pay for what you are ready to sell, there is disconnect between price and affordability. Hence, no transaction takes place.

In economics, this is called lack of "effective demand". Effective demand; to put it simply, is defined as wants, needs, and desires backed by the *ability to pay*. Assuming other factors remain the same and the prices of real estate are high, making it unaffordable, then prices directly lend to the buyer's "inability to pay". This would mean that there is a lack of effective demand.

So, one of the prerequisites of selling is that there should BE **EFFECTIVE DEMAND**. We shall keep this term in mind as we go forward.

The 'SUBDIVISION Effect':

Democratization of land

In India during the 1980s, and later that decade the construction cost of a house was far more than the price of land itself. However, with the real estate market slowly picking up property prices in the Metro cities in India began to slowly increase in value only towards the end of the decade.

In those days the market was purely driven by true end user demand and supply. Interestingly, hence in cities like Chennai, Bengaluru and Hyderabad, having a home meant having an independent house. People who could afford independent homes and apartments were fewer in number. This, however, began to change as land prices began to firm up and rise. One factor driving this change was the Subdivision Effect.

What is subdivision effect? Subdivision Effect is one of the major factors affecting real estate, especially in India. This is particularly so where factors like effective demand, lack of housing and desire of people to own their own home is predominant. Before explaining subdivision effect in real estate terms, I will talk from the perspective of stocks and shares. Let us assume that the price of an equity stock is Rs. 800/- per share in the stock market. Say for theory's sake, a company announces a stock split of 8-for-1. Now the price of the stock would be Rs. 100/- per share and a person who had one share valued at Rupees 800 now has 8 shares valued at Rs. 100 each. The capitalization of the stock remains the same. Rupees 100 multiplied by eight would equal Rupees eight hundred (100 x 8=800). Only it has just been split up.

Why then did the company split the shares? That's because it wanted the stock to be more liquid. More people could now afford the stock. There are more investors with the capacity to pay Rs. 100/- per share, rather than Rs. 800/- per share. When the ticket size is smaller more people could own shares at Rs. 100/-per share. This in practice means that the effective demand has increased as far as the market is concerned.

The effective stock price actually rises in practice though a lot of market analysts dispute the theory. It makes sense to dispute this theory in the stock market as we know that irrespective of whether the stock is split or not, the total earning of the company remains the same and so does its market capitalization.

The Price per Earnings (P/E) multiple of the stock is not going to change overnight just because the shares were split. Thus, theoretically share price should not rise. However, it does rise a bit in practice. This can be attributed to effective demand rising because the stock became affordable to a larger subset of people.

If I draw the same parallel with real estate, let's assume there is a property valued at Rs. 8 Crores. Now if we subdivide it into 8 parts each valued at Rupees One Crore; we increase the EFFECTIVE demand as the number of persons able to afford that price tag and the subset of buyers increase. (As opposed to the number of persons who may be able to afford properties at the price of Rupees Eight Crores.)

Now, if we apply the subdivision effect, EACH of the eight parts would actually sell for a sum greater than the One Crore of money we started out with. This is because the subdivision has caused a greater number of people to be included in the subset of the buyers, altering the supply-demand dynamics and creating greater effective demand

Applying this subdivision effect to real estate, whether you consider acreages converted to plots or plots converted to apartments, subdivision effect works in all cases.

Let us assume you have a plot of land with a house on it. The value of the house may be different from the value of the land. The land may be in a location that may fetch an expensive price. When you would go to the market to sell it, you would find it difficult to move the sale. This is not because your house and plot are undesirable. In fact, a number of people would give an arm and a leg to own such a property.

The problem is that your set of prospective buyers with such a high purchasing power is quite small as the price of premium land is too expensive for many. Here, you are facing a classic case of lack of effective demand. Everyone would agree that your piece of real estate is very valuable. However, few would be able to come forward to buy it.

What would a builder do in this example? A builder would bring out a proposal to demolish the house and build, for instance 8 apartments in its place (assuming the permissible Floor Space Index FSI (FAR) and number of kitchen restrictions of 8 kitchens per apartment block being allowed). Once you would agree he may buy you out and begin construction. (For this example, to simply explain subdivision effect, the complexities of Joint Venture Development and other scenarios have been excluded.) The builder would construct the eight apartments as proposed.

Interestingly, the number of prospective buyers the builder is able to capture would be more than what you would have initially been able to attract, even though the builder's price per square foot may be higher than what you may have quoted.

It is highly possible he is selling the pieces of land at a sum greater than the whole. If your price was "X", he would sell each of the 8 apartments at X/8 plus a PREMIUM (due to subdivision effect) + construction cost + his profits. So, despite the sum of the selling price of his eight parts of land being greater than the original price you asked for, he is able to make an easy sale while you struggled. In other words, the land component of what he sold is 8X + Plus Premium + His profit without including the construction cost. Therefore, the sum of his eight parts in value sold as land is greater than the original price you quoted.

By dividing the property into smaller-parts the builder has made a premium property affordable to many more by increasing the set of people to whom he can sell. He has basically increased your subset of buyers and thereby drawn liquidity into the system where there was none before.

Now more money has flowed into the real estate space. New buyers have allocated their savings into this space. Having seen this success, a new builder will pitch in a price for your neighbour's property but this time at a higher price than what was paid for yours. This would continue as the land price increases at a brisk rate even as you watch.

This effect is the subdivision effect or in other words it is the democratization of land. Here more people are buying land subdivided into smaller pieces. The price of such land would continue increasing as long as the demand for such land continues to grow in this market. This in turn increases the supply of money in the system further pushing up prices.

Whether this actually happens in the stock market is debatable, but it definitely happens in the real estate market. The splitting of land into plots or conversion of homes into flats/apartments injects liquidity into the system and brings in fresh money which causes the prices to go up.

It can be argued that in the stock market the effect can be questioned because the net capitalization stocks can be easily valued against parameters such as cash flows etc., and therefore splitting should not have increased capitalization of the stock.

However, the effect is more pronounced in the real estate sector as we are dealing with huge sums and any subdivision (or undivided share as you may call it) causes a huge injection of liquidity and more people being included to play their savings in the system causes greater effective demand and the consequent price rise. Effective demand is a more potent factor in real estate than in stock market because of the sheer ticket sizes involved.

Often in the outskirts of cities where demand for real estate is climbing, we see huge parcels of land being converted to plots. These lands are usually sold at a per acre rate. However, when these lands are converted to plots and sold, the added value of the smaller plots would be more than the total value of the price per acre.

One of the effects that would increase the number of buyers of subdivided land is the democratization of land effecting affordability. The subdivision effect can be seen even here. The subdivision effect happens both in plotting of acreages as well as in building of apartments. Such democratization of land increases effective demand altering the supply demand equation and increasing the price.

Hence, we can say with the coming of apartments the plot prices do invariably jump and with the coming of plots in the outskirts the land prices move in an upward trajectory.

The 'EMI Effect'

So far, we have seen how subdivision effect increased the effective demand and thereby altered the demand supply situation to cause increased prices. Let us see another factor that has caused the increase in prices in a short duration. The answer lies in what the government did. It eased lending norms and allowed housing loans to come into being.

Cheap financing along with Fiscal incentives (tax deductions) on payment of interest and repayment of principal have fuelled the EMI effect. EMI – Equal Monthly Instalments, a buyer could buy property with down payment and a bank loan; and pay off the loan in Equal Monthly Instalments over time.

Now one can buy with not only one's savings but also with one's prospective future earnings. This brought about an abrupt radical change as it caused the injection of liquidity into the real estate eco-system.

A number of people have benefitted from this. A number of first-time home buyers have been able to buy their first property because of the lending policy. It enabled many with the purchasing power, and increased effective demand which was further fuelled by subdivision effect.

However, the EMI effect which has caused more affordability by introducing the time factor (where one could pay back over time) has had some unintended consequences too. It has caused a sudden spurt in effective demand without the supply side issues being sorted out.

We shall go into some of the supply side issues later. It suffices to say that people can afford to pay more for a property than they could have before, because of the lending policy. This immediately induces liquidity in the market which results in real estate prices rising.

The 'GROWTH Effect'

In a period from the late 1990s until now the Indian economy has grown at an appreciable pace. The middle class has expanded vastly and so have their incomes and desires. Their desire and dream of owning a home have taken roots. Increased incomes mean increased affordability and therefore increased prices. Urbanization and migration from rural to urban areas have fuelled the growth effect.

We have to note here that even small increases in income in a short duration could cause a huge jump in property prices. For example, let's suppose a person earns a disposable income of Rupees 10,000/month more than the previous year. Presuming he could invest the entire sum in real estate, he could probably afford a mortgage of Rupees 8-10 lakhs more than he did the previous year. His purchasing power has multiplied many times his salary.

It is another story that the person would need to pay up Rs. 10,000 extra every month for the next 20 years. People rarely think that far. They are driven by the fear that prices would rise further and also by the greed that they could profit tremendously. Often the instincts of fear and greed combined, force many to commit their increased future salary to EMI. This trend affects the supply demand equation in the market forcing the escalation of the price of real estate.

This brings us to our next factor which I call the Max out Effect.

The 'MAX-OUT Effect'

'Equilibrium' at the Higher End of Spectrum

What is the Max out Effect? This is a rather sinister effect. It can be stated that, "the price a consumer ends up paying for a property is often the HIGHEST that he was WILLING to pay".

We all know that in India people have intense desires to own a home. My grandmother once said "we should have a roof over our heads which is our own. We may even be drinking a meagre porridge under that roof. Yet it would be ours, besides, who would know what we do within the confines of our *own* home?" Such was the determination and desire to have a place of one's own. Owning a home meant everything. In the days of my grandmother's generation, people would spend their entire life time savings to build their dream house. Many typical middle-class people like my grandfather saved all through their life and built their home after retirement.

Now, coming back to Max out Effect. The price of a home would often be one that would stretch your budget to the maximum. After all a home is a necessity and the only thing holding you back is the affordability. The moment the effective demand in the market rises, immediately the price also rises to fill in the void. It is a game of changing goal posts. In this regard, it is rather baleful.

The industry and economy would max you out before you could buy a home. This is one of the reasons why buying a home seems just out of reach even though your income has risen and EMIs have been introduced.

Even as liquidity and affordability are ushered in, the goal post represented by the prices just keeps moving out of reach. Once upon a time a house even on acreage was something people could dream about, nowadays it's unimaginable.

We also should take note that while people's salaries have increased (growth effect) and their potential to pay has increased (EMI effect) prices of homes have always been a little more than what can be afforded by them. The market has to offer smaller and smaller properties (Subdivision effect) at larger and increasing prices.

Please note that this is not just because of inflation alone. It is all these effects which have been explained in the previous pages that have caused the land inflation in the first place. Despite all these factors the builders (and land owner) are charging you the max you can afford for a piece of real estate because of what I call "Max out Effect". This is often done by what in real estate is called 'Price discovery'.

What is 'Price discovery'? Usually, builders do not know what is the highest price they could quote for a property, they may do market mapping. Market mapping is to scout the region within which their property is and find the going rate in that region. Rather than just quoting a price after adding in a reasonable profit for themselves, they find the best price to sell at.

Hence when a builder suddenly quotes a higher price in a location, and the market responds positively, all builders and land owners would increase the price of the real estate in tandem at once. The prices move to a new equilibrium. They have basically discovered the maximum you are willing to shell out. It's the max out effect in full bloom.

To explain this better, consider the Average Joe could afford only 100 units of money to buy an average property in an average city. The lack of effective demand here would normally have kept the price of that property at 100 units. The price of the property would have been 100 units. As the average purchasing power is at 100 units, many would evince their interest in such a purchase.

The suppliers in the real estate market are fully aware of the purchasing power of the average buyer. Assume now the Average Joe could spare 200 units of money. When many more join Joe to buy more property similar to Joe's, would the market still quote 100 units for the same piece of real-estate? The answer is 'no'. They will increase the price to the maximum, without any increase in the intrinsic value of the property.

The suppliers have only "discovered the price" affordable by the buyer. With this discovery they constantly maximize the price of real estate. This is the max out effect. Housing is a necessity and one will be charged the maximum one can afford for it. The equilibrium of the price will always be at the higher end of the spectrum.

The subdivision effect, growth effect and EMI effect have created such a demand in the short term without being matched by supply that all one can afford today is something in the outskirts in smaller units. Hence one actually pays more and more money for less and less real estate.

Nothing will easily change this. The real estate industry will charge the maximum one can pay for the necessity - the home - and the land owners are going to charge the builders the max they can all derive from one's effective demand, which comes from the Subdivision effect, EMI effect and the growth effect put together.

As owning a home is a necessity, the real estate market offers one smaller and smaller homes that one could "afford". The market is constantly giving you options that are just out of your reach. "If a house in a large plot is too expensive for you, how about a smaller independent one with a small garden? Is that too expensive? Then probably we shall sell you a nice apartment with 3 – 4 (BHK) Bedrooms, a Hall and Kitchen in the city? Is that outside your budget? If so, how about a 3 BHK apartment in the suburbs of the city? Even if this is too expensive, we shall sell you a 2 BHK apartment in the outskirts with smaller rooms and half the square feet area." This is how the market treats one nowadays even as one's income and affordability increases.

The combination of subdivision effect, the growth effect, and EMI effect etc., together with the max out effect cause one to afford smaller areas, further and further away even though the prices are just increasing. The question is when will it stop? We shall discuss that and more as we go along in this book.

The market is evolving as it constantly tries all the tricks in the book to sell one real estate. First it tried subdivision of large parcels of land, then subdivision of houses into apartments. When this was exhausted the market churned out apartments in the suburbs. No doubt there is need based demand that is affecting the supply, however the prices quoted are often "maxed out" making one spend all out in the purchase of the property.

Hence, it is converting the effective demand into various other kinds of products that individuals are forced to spend all their resources on. When even an apartment in the suburbs of the city becomes unaffordable the market would max-out and sell smaller units in the outskirts.

Notice how from your grandfather's time your affordability has actually decreased. The middle class has been pushed from houses to apartments of smaller units in the outskirts.

It is to be noted that during the 1980s the cost of a building was far greater than the corresponding piece of land in a typical city like Bengaluru or Chennai. However now, though construction costs have increased; the cost of land far outweighs a building in the cities.

If the government would increase the permissible Floor Space Index FSI (FAR) in primary areas of a city would that decrease the prices? The answer is 'no' again.

In the long term the builders would still charge one the max one can pay and give the SAME apartment at the SAME price with a smaller slice of undivided share (UDS) of land, and that would be all. Interestingly following this one would see that this would only cause an increase in land prices and not a decrease in apartment rates.

The rates for apartments would still be at their same per square foot rate, but greater built-up area on the same parcel of land permitted by greater FSI (FAR) would mean that the land value has been quietly given a shot in the arm without it benefitting the end consumer.

It would be unfortunate that one would have to pay the same amount for the same apartment but get a smaller undivided share of land. This phenomenon is because of the max out effect.

The 'FRESH MONEY Effect'

"Fresh money effect" is another factor that causes higher real estate prices. When customers come to believe that it is profitable to invest in real estate, they begin to allocate more of the investable funds in real estate. This causes an increase in liquidity in the real estate market. In other words, fresh money from savings and other instruments are diverted into real estate and stays there. This keeps the price of real estate escalating.

Many have moved their invested funds from other sectors to real estate. My friend Varghese had a balanced portfolio with investments fairly divided in shares, bonds, real estate and gold.

His portfolio was balanced until 2008 struck. The value of his shares plunged and so did his faith in them. Even then he held on. A few years went by and gold increased with the quantitative easing by the US. Finally, around 2013 gold prices almost peaked and dipped slightly.

Varghese reviewed how well his portfolio had done. He found that his investment in Shares had done badly. Investments in gold had done well, however it did not seem like it would rise further.

He then noticed that the investments in real estate had done very well, and he had managed a nice fortune from its sale. Varghese then reinvested his profits in real estate as he found no other that was as profitable. He also went on to withdraw all his money from the stock market. He was unable to take the volatility and invested the proceeds in real estate.

Now this is an example where fresh money moved into real estate and was allocated from other sectors of investment. Such moves are commonplace, as people in India have constantly held the belief that the value of real estate would not fall so easily and is more likely to increase.

This effect where your real estate allocation constantly rises in the investor's portfolio is the 'Fresh money effect'. Even as investment in real estate re-circulates within the sector as the investments are bought and sold, fresh money from other sectors moves into this sector. This is because people believe strongly that real estate is a safe haven.

The 'INFRASTRUCTURE DEFICIENCY Effect'

In the early '90s, much before the real estate boom, my father was driving through bad roads to drop me at high school. The neighbourhood was actually the heart of the city, yet it had the one of the most potholed roads in the city. My dad said, "I can't believe that a neighbourhood with such high property prices has such bad roads". Many years later I thought about this and really wondered about the question. "Why was the infrastructure so poor while the prices continue to be so high?

I thought about it for some time and then the realization dawned. Maybe the question was wrongly framed and the key to puzzle was in the question itself. The question to ask was; 'Is bad infrastructure the reason for high prices in the first place?'

It may sound like a sore note in a beautiful melody, but it's actually one of the reasons for high property prices. Here I am not talking about the bad roads that I was driving through, but the lack of proper infrastructure and public utilities everywhere which actually lends to higher property prices. Yes, low property taxes were one of the reasons for poor infrastructure. However, that does not explain why property prices were so high in relation to income earned. The answer was poor infrastructure has curtailed the supply side of the equation and pushed up prices.

If India had a good transportation network in the form of metro trains, super highways and the supply of land was kept high, the chances of the prices settling at a higher equilibrium would be less. More people would be able to live even further from their place of work and yet be able to commute in comfort. This would have kept the supply side of the equation going even as the demand kept rising continuously.

The upward effect that an infrastructure deficiency has on land prices can be termed as 'Infrastructure deficiency effect'.

Some people may argue that Mumbai and Delhi, despite having good transportation networks compared to other cities, have soaring prices in real estate. What one fails to see is that the transportation networks in these cities are not sufficient enough to cater to their huge populations.

The answer to most woes would be in the creation of satellite townships around cities which would have kept the prices of land in check. Imagine the price of estates in Delhi if not for Gurgaon or Noida. There would have been severe congestion over ten times of what it is today.

It is to be further noted that in cities like Delhi and Mumbai the subdivision effect, the growth effect, the EMI effect and the max out effect significantly contribute to the real estate prices as these places are centres of economic activity. In addition, the turnover of land deals in these places are very high.

It may seem like the chapter speaks of only problems without any solution, but as I explain more into the book, I will elaborate on my understanding of the problems in the system and what may be suitable solutions.

The 'BUREAUCRATIC Effect'

Slow Approval Processes:

During the 70s, a quality revolution quietly took place in Japan. Car companies applied quality control measures as proposed by Mr. Edward Deming. A number of tools related to Statistical process control (SPC) and design of experiments (DOE) were used to root out quality problems in the production of cars. Apart from these ideas of quality one idea that caught their fancy that was very effective was the principle of just-in-time (JIT) manufacturing. It was developed by the founder of Toyota, Sakichi Toyoda. The idea fundamentally sought to maintain a lean inventory system, consequently keeping low working capitals to keep business efficient.

The result of JIT was that production costs were brought down while the time for production got minimized. The important take away for us from this is that the working capital was kept to a minimum and was tied up for the least time before production commenced, bringing down the final cost of the product.

If we draw an analogy in real estate, we would need to study the various building blocks that go in to the production of housing and apartments. One of the primary requisites in building and construction are plans which require approval from the Urban Development Authorities, City Corporations and other governing bodies. Approvals form a significant part of time delays in the projects; tying the investments down and for want of quick approvals it probably adds 10-15% to the cost of a project. This bureaucratic delay is very costly for builders, indirectly affecting the public in terms of price. It is hard to understand why the government cannot expand the number of people employed in the approval granting bodies in the cities. Why not modernize them make them technology savvy, increase work force and improve time to market?

These will not only help builders to reduce cost, but will also allow them to react to market demands quickly and keep prices low. After all the supply-demand dynamics does affect price. Therefore, it is imperative to help the industry with quick approval turnarounds to keep the end cost of the product minimum. Not only this, it would also lead to good employment generation and a thriving economy.

The 'STACK ON Effect'

The 'Sell and Buy' effect

In the United States of America people have a certain financial pattern to their lives. Teenagers leave home when they are 18 years old and live on their own. They take out an education loan, study, and graduate and then try for a job. Immediately on getting a job they first buy a car by taking a car loan, and finally live the great American dream, which is to own a home.

They take a home loan and buy their dream house. They then raise a family and when their children become 18+ and they leave their nests. The parents in the meanwhile work until retirement as they pay off the house.

On retirement the couple would often sell off their home and cash in the equity. They then would move into retirement homes. Their kids in the meanwhile go on to live a similar financial life cycle. At least this used to be the plan for the majority of folks of the baby boomer generation.

Shifting focus to India. The middle class in the cities bought their homes during the 60s, 70s, 80s and 90s and formed the cities that we see today. This population then raised children and has passed on the inheritance to them or is in the process of doing so. Unlike their western counterparts the Indian parents were often supported by their children and in return were left properties.

This has led to an unusual effect which I call the "stack on effect". The children of these parents who were born in the 70s, 80s and even 90s did not have to start from scratch unlike most of their parents.

This older generation neither had credit or loans to buy property and heavily disliked debt. They worked their entire lives saving for a property and at the time of their retirement they went on to build or buy one.

Their children went to on to inherit these and any additional wealth. This they would use as down payment when they wanted to buy a property of their own. They could pay their EMIs on any excess amount required for the property even if the cost was beyond the money they paid for down payment. The down payment often came from the ancestral property they sold.

In effect the idea was, either keep the ancestral property and live in it or sell that property and buy a new home often by bridging the excess required by using EMIs. This is the "stack on effect", when children choose to buy new or larger properties, by using the stacked wealth inherited from an ancestral property sold.

Unlike in the US where the generation of children going in to adulthood generally had to start from scratch, the Indian middle-class children most often began with an inheritance, which meant that they could pay higher prices. By applying the max-out effect they land up paying larger sums for city properties and kept the effective demand going.

The net effect is that the prices in the cities bear no relationship to the average incomes. This is one of the major reasons why the real estate prices are so high in prime central areas of the city. Since most of them are inherited properties, the sell and buy effect is in play. People are able to afford higher prices even though their incomes alone would not normally make the cut.

The 'BLACK MONEY Effect'

Parallel Economy

Finally, I would like to state one more major reason for high real estate prices. This is to do with the parallel economy. Money that evades taxes is often in common parlance called black money. This could have been generated in business, via corruption, criminal activities or other black money transactions.

Whatever its source one of the best ways to tuck away the cash happens to be real estate. This flow of cash keeps the real estate prices at unreasonable levels. By introducing circle rates (guideline values) in the past, the Government has tried to curb black money with limited success.

As long as there is corruption and businesses are forced to deal in cash to get permits, licenses or keep their businesses lubricated, black money and artificially high real estate prices would continue to remain.

The 'GOVERNMENT POLICY Effect'

Government policy can play a major role in affecting real estate prices. The Indian property market took off since March 2005 when the current government headed United Progressive Alliance (UPA) decided to liberalize foreign direct investment norms in real estate on Feb 26, 2005; introduced the Special Economic Zone (SEZ) Act in 2005; and allowed private equity funds into real estate.

The flow of foreign funds has propelled the real estate prices resulting in increases in prices of urban land and property.

Hence government policies can also affect the real estate prices. Good inflows in the form of FDIs and private equity would mean greater investment inflows and uses for land that was previously under-utilized.

The new money flowing in causes real estate prices to rise.

CONCLUSION

In this chapter we have analysed the obvious and non-obvious factors which have caused and continue to cause the real estate prices to be out of reach.

While some of these factors would have obvious to one, some other factors could have been a surprise. There are a lot more factors that affect the price of a home and other real estate offerings.

This chapter is meant to be an eye opener for the reader to take his/her thought process a little deeper so that they at least have a better idea what they are paying for when they purchase.

Chapter 6

WHEN IS IT A BUBBLE IN THE REAL ESTATE?

How to recognize a Bubble in Real Estate

"For every bubble,
a pin awaits."

- *Warren Buffet*

"The precondition for a bubble is intense belief without any possibility of questioning."

- *Michael Ellsberg,*
The Education of Millionaires

Recently, I was in one of India's Metro cities, driving down its newly laid highway. I couldn't help but admire the tall high rises that were sprouting up on either side of that highway. I had been down the same highway three years ago; it was a revelation when I had driven through this time.

The half-constructed buildings were now complete and there were a lot more now that were tall, impressive and very modern. In a span of three years the place had transformed with spanking new buildings everywhere.

I was very impressed with many of the upcoming buildings and even contemplated buying some property in the region. "After all," I deduced, "If many builders were building here, these properties must be set up for terrific appreciation. There must be great demand and there were good chances of making a killing." While I drove past these buildings toward my destination, I made a quick calculation and a mental note.

I finally reached my destination and completed my work and drove back via the same highway. This time however, it was after nightfall. As I drove through this newly laid out corridor with it's large structures and extraordinary construction, I was struck with an eerie feeling. The stretch seemed deserted, though it boasted of many new office and residential spaces.

As I gazed up to see the facades of some of the finished towers, I was surprised to notice they were not lit, showing that many were unoccupied. It was possible that they had been sold but were without tenants or, worse yet, they were probably unsold. These were signs that had me doubt my previous assessment. I had second thoughts and concluded that maybe it did not have a great investment potential after all.

In India, the best way to judge how well a completed project fares, is to drive through that project or property at night. If the properties are illuminated, with cars parked and other signs of occupation, we know they have been sold and tenants or end users are using them. This is normally a good sign.

However, if they are not lit and unoccupied then maybe there is little or no effective demand for the project as yet. Otherwise, it could also be that these projects have been sold, and the new owners have not found tenants. These are both worrying signs for the future.

At the end of 2012; China had close to 64 million; empty apartments. This is a definitive sign of a bubble brewing. The Chinese, like Indians, generally have very few avenues to invest their surplus money and a number of them end up in the property market buying apartments that nobody wants or uses.

Generally, one of the signs of a bubble is the number of vacant apartments.

A large number of empty and locked up residential and commercial units are normally a bad sign for the economy and real estate sector. This, when combined with high property prices, often tells you that a crash is due. However, it is difficult to predict the tipping point or the timing of the crash.

To complete my story of my drive down the highway, I could not help but wonder if this was the beginning of a bubble or would the demand catch up to the stock being held in the market?

Signs of a Bubble?

A bubble just does not happen in a day. A bubble brews for a while. It begins with speculation-fuelled rise in demand and prices, which would have more people joining in, furthering the bubble influence; this could then cause a snowball effect. More rational people are sucked in and become irrational.

More and more people continue to invest even as it becomes clear to the rest of the sensible folks that such investment may not be sustainable.

Actually, this trend would continue for quite a while. Many investors would liquidate their other savings and allot them to real estate, until, it becomes their major investment and sometimes it is their only holding.

Sometimes certain people who would make profits at the peak with quick buys and sales would even be convincing themselves and others that this is the best investment and best time to invest.

One could be such a speculative investor at the pick, and it may be fine as long as one gets out before the bubble bursts. Until then it may even work favourably as a means of making money. However, one should not delude oneself into believing that the investment was not risky or worth it.

It should be a conscious call that the investment would be speculative and risky and mostly short term. One should try to get out without being too greedy. It is to be noted that no one can predict when a bubble will burst or when the slide would happen.

Uday Kulkarni, a gentleman in Mumbai liquidated all his investments in stocks in 2011. Prior to that year the stock market had not done well for over 3 years. So, he invested all his liquidated funds in commercial real estate.

He was advised wrongly and his due diligence on such an investment was poor; his stocks were now properties that were not yielding rent as he couldn't find any tenant.

As of early 2013 Uday had continued to hold these properties which unfortunately had also dipped in value. Though there was no dramatic bubble burst, there was a significant slowdown. Kulkarni's property investment was in limbo; it was not earning him anything through rent and was slowly dropping in value.

It may be that it would have been a temporary blip in the real estate market, but it however does not justify him liquidating his stock portfolio. To put all eggs in one basket while real estate prices are high, in the hope prices would rise further, is a rather risky move.

In truth, as of 2012, a real estate crash has never happened in India. However, it does not mean that it could not happen. It's important to note that even if real estate prices are stagnant for a few years, we would need to take into account inflation.

One should consider the particular investment in real estate to have gone down in value quite a bit as inflation would cause a dip in the value of money. In India even stagnation is to be considered as a downward movement bearing in mind the inflation in the economy.

A real estate bubble does not burst like a stock market bubble where there is a crash in a period as short as a day. There are no 'Black Mondays' like on Oct 19, 1987 or 'Black Tuesdays' as in the Wall Street Crash of 1929.

There was a single day crash in the markets on both these dates. Real estate market crashes would typically happen over a period of time, say 6 months to a year.

This is primarily because the number of transactions in the market is fewer when compared to the humungous number of transactions at the stock market.

Since one transaction leads to a reaction in another following transaction, a crash would not occur in a day, unless there are many such transactions in such a short duration. There is not a flurry of transactions leading to a crash. It is often slow and deliberate.

Moreover, the signs of a crash may appear much before the slide and may be spotted by some. It is just that it is difficult to predict exactly when the slide accelerates.

When it does get noticed, it seems to have happened all of a sudden. Here are a number of signs that crop up leading up to a crash.

Some of the signs to look out for are:

1) High Price-to-Income Ratio:

When the price of the real estate becomes much higher than 3 to 5 multiples of the annual income of the target-customers we can say we are entering a speculative territory. Normally what we are looking for here is affordability and a constant stream of properties being absorbed in the market. This can happen only if the income has a favourable relationship to price of the property. If divergence between the two is significant, then we are heading for an expensive market. Typically, any further increase in price is not justifiable. We can say we are entering a speculative phase which precedes a bubble.

Conversely, if incomes are constantly rising, then high prices may be justified. So, when the economy grows rapidly, incomes also grow and higher prices can be justified to some extent. This ratio accommodates for that.

Another factor that needs to be highlighted is the 'stack on' effect. The 'stack on' effect as described in preceding chapters justifies high prices of property even for modest income levels keeping this ratio high. So, this is something unique to India and an aspect that one has to bear in mind.

2) Low Rent to Price Ratio Percentage:

This ratio denotes the rent that a property of a certain price would fetch. This factor is also called rental yield. Rental yields vary from market to market and depend on local economic conditions, ease of ownership of property, availability of units and number of other factors.

Historically, rental yields in Singapore have been 3-4%, while in Kuala Lumpur it has been 8-9%. In India, rental yields are poor and in the range of 2-3% and is similar to China.

Rental yields in India, 9-10 years ago were much higher and have steeply declined since then. Poor rental yields denote that the prices in the market are on the higher side.

It shows properties are not fetching adequate return which makes them a poor investment. This highlights a poor investors' market.

Rental yields however cannot be seen in isolation and have to be seen in the light of returns from other investment opportunities or opportunity costs. Also, rental yields may not factor in possible future capital appreciation in properties. It denotes the 'now' scenario.

This 'now' scenario is dynamic and can change with the economy. If the economy grows, then incomes may rise and account for greater rent potential and better rental yield.

Conversely if the situation of the economy is such that it does not grow, any sudden rise in property prices, without commensurate increase in rent could cause a fall in the corresponding rental yields.

This would definitely expose the fact that the property price rise is not on a firm footing and is lacking in strong foundation. It needs to be accompanied by rising rentals if it is to be justified.

3) Vacancies:

Generally poor occupancy of properties does indicate an imminent bubble. Even if the properties are selling initially, high vacancies can be the early signs of a problem. When the properties turn out to be dead investments and it could result in stagnation of the value of property.

At some point this would make investors ask fundamental questions relating to returns on investment. Normally purchases that are speculative in nature are done with the intention of selling the property to the next bidder at a higher price. This speculation is the fundamental initiator of a bubble.

When the buyers stop believing in the story of a fortune that could possibly be made, the bubble begins to wobble and a crash is instigated. High number of vacancies and high property prices are the precursors for a bubble burst. These are vital signs that one needs to watch out for.

4) Rent Vs EMI Divergence:

Owning a home normally should be cheaper than renting one. This should be so because with the decision to own a home one gives up certain options.

The primary option one gives up is the flexibility of location, which could vary with one's place of work. In case of a commercial establishment too, it should be cheaper to own one.

By buying the property, the business gives up the flexibility to relocate to locations where the business may thrive better. Normally, for this reason in many places outside of India owning a home/commercial property is cheaper.

However, in India the economy is growing at a rapid pace. Property values could be high in the expectation of further escalation in values as the economy grows and incomes rises. Hence the property prices and corresponding EMIs are higher when benchmarked against rent for the same property.

This should normally not be a problem, however when there is a great divergence between EMIs and rent and this divergence is increasing at a snowballing rate then we are setting ourselves up in an unviable territory. It may indicate a bubble especially if the economy tanks.

5) Share of Residential Housing Investment as a Share of GDP:

When the share of residential housing investment as a share of GDP increases sharply from the historical averages this is an indicator that the Housing buildup has grown much more relative to the economy as a whole. It tells us that housing has gone ahead of the economy.

In other words, the housing buildup has gone ahead of what the economy can absorb. For instance, in China this ratio grew from 2% in 2000 to 6% in 2011. This is indicative of lopsided growth and a spurt in residential housing. This is another factor therefore which needs to be studied and deliberated on.

6) Number of Secondary Housing Sales to Primary:

When a property is bought from the developer or builder the sale is considered a primary sale. The subsequent sale of the property is termed as secondary sales.

If the number of secondary housing sales to primary is low, this could be an indicator of lack of underlying demand. This lack of demand from original end users could point to a bubble.

Normally, investors tend to buy property-in-construction and dabble in the primary market. The primary market is normally the market where speculators make their money.

End users dabble in both primary and secondary market. Absence of end users from the secondary market is generally a very poor sign for the market. It is akin to a missing leg of a table.

When secondary market purchases are slower than primary and the secondary market is weak it indicates that speculators are buying up new properties at a much faster rate. It indicates that it is being hoarded and not being offloaded to the end user.

The stock is then growing in the market without end users. Under normal circumstances, the primary and secondary markets grow in tandem and complement each other. If and when this does not happen and the primary demand far outstrips the secondary demand, we are in bubble territory.

7) Lack of Liquidity in the Market:

When the investor classes are asset rich and cash poor, we are setting ourselves up for a bubble. In the lead up to a bubble, speculators buy much of the in-construction properties. Property developers then lock in the customers by raising prices. The early investors have notional gains and are happy but prices have risen without justification. Investors then wait to offload the properties. This is when liquidity is low and investors are asset rich and cash poor. Offloading of properties then gets difficult.

Builders also sell properties to other intermediaries and assign them to brokers. They then put out the 'sold out' board. The brokers then resell the properties in the midst of the enthusiasm generated for the property by the 'sold out' boards. This happens until a time when the speculators and investors hold most of the stock. They have notional gains but no liquidity. When they need liquidity, they become desperate and the drop in prices begins to take hold. Also, when it becomes unviable to flip properties, it would lead to a crash in the market.

Timing of a 'Bubble Burst'

Only in retrospect does one identify or recognize that a bubble has burst. It is nearly impossible to predict when a bubble will rupture. Generally, when parameters are getting out of line, if we step back, we can say that we are in speculative territory. Normally that can even be alright as the economy sometimes catches up with high property prices as incomes rise.

However, it is to be noted that this does not happen always. A speculative phase precedes a bubble phase. It is then that we enter the region of over speculation. Here the markets get carried away and rides on irrationality.

A lot of rational people who stayed away during the speculative phase may feel they have missed out and re-enter. The bubble grows feeding on itself. A lot of irrationality is then rife in the market.

A crash generally happens when some of the irrational people playing in the market suddenly begin turning rational and asking fundamental questions. This happens when technical analysis which was the basis of their purchases until then, no more works when the market stagnates.

At this time, fundamental questions relating to rental yield, growth in rentals, number of vacant unused apartments in the market, lack of affordability, etc., begin to crop up. It becomes obvious that the game is up. The number of players willing to play the game dwindles and a crash is initiated.

Warren Buffett once said,

"It is only when the tide goes out
do you discover
who's been swimming naked."

To look at the build up to a bubble let us take the example of the subprime crisis in the US in the year 2008. Here we study the 'Monthly Rent Vs Monthly Mortgage Payment' chart and the 'Home Inventory Position'.

The figure below taken from JP Morgan Asset Management gives a snap shot of the Monthly rent Vs Monthly Mortgage Payment over a 25-year period.

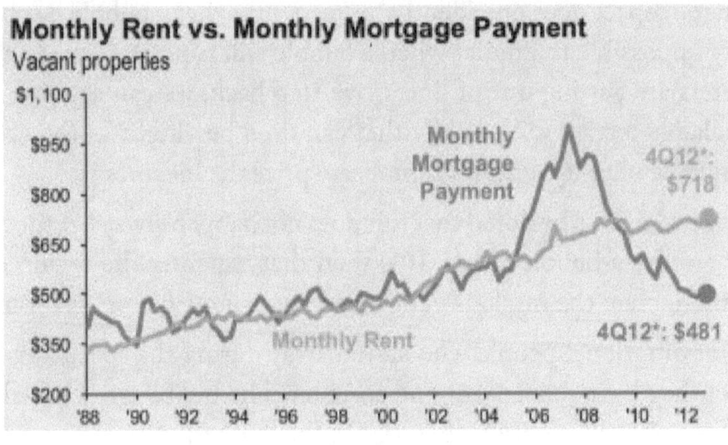

Fig 8.1

From the graph Fig 8.1 it can be seen that since 2006 the average EMI payment far outstripped the rent that a similar property would fetch. Moreover, until a time almost to 2008 this divergence grew larger.

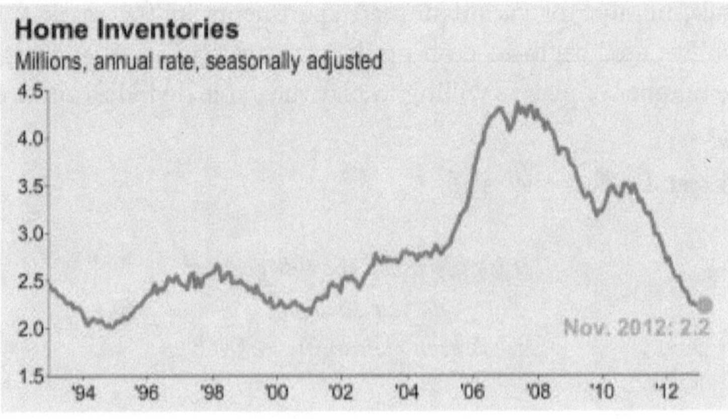

Fig 8.2

The indicators grew shriller. The further thing to be noted is that during the Phase of 2007-08 the home inventories were at their highest.

The inventories and high property prices pointed to the fact that a bubble was forming. Then, came the pin to prick the bubble.

There was the subprime crisis of 2008 and everything came to a halt with an implosion. The bubble had been pricked. The bubble collapsed leaving the market in tatters and a lot of lives in shambles.

Consider the rent as being the basis for a fundamental analysis and the price a person ends up paying as EMI as the basis for the technical analysis; in a bubble, the graph of the EMI and rent would begin to tell you a lot.

When the technical analysis of a property (i.e. the price of the property represented by the EMI) breaks away from the fundamental analysis (as represented by the rent the property could fetch) and when they diverge to a great extent, we can confidently say that the property prices are not on a sound footing and we have entered speculative territory.

This divergence can be seen in Fig 8.1 from 2006 adding up to year 2008. This speculative territory is pretty enticing and will suck in a lot of good folks looking to invest.

The market will move from an end user's market into a market where investors bet heavily. This will cause prices to rise sharply. This rise will be devoid of the support of fundamentals.

Going further the prices will be unjustifiable and the inventories will begin to pile up. All this does not happen in a day and the rational investors will sense a bubble.

Greed can often keep us from seeing a bubble and even rational investors can get sucked in and tend to hold on. The bubble could build and build and build and take a long time before it bursts. In the meantime, a lot of fortunes are made by those who exit. Finally, the bubble bursts.

In India even a stagnation considering the inflation is a sign that the market is cooling. Normally it is best therefore to exit when one feels uncomfortable with the prices, unless one is a very long-term investor or is buying a home for one's self.

So, generally apart from watching all the indicators that we have discussed in the chapter we need to make sure that the divergence between the technical analysis and fundamental analysis of the property is not widening at an increasingly rapid rate. This could point to a bubble.

The only point where this divergence would be justified is when the economy is growing at a blistering pace and the lag in fundamental analysis would be bridged with time and quickly as the rents rise with the expanding economy.

So, basically the fundamental analysis should catch up with the technical analysis. The pace of growth of the economy in such a scenario is the key. Failing this, the technical analysis would end up being mere speculation and hot air.

So, you really have to take that call on a case-by-case basis. Now you are better equipped to take that call. Considering you are in most cases putting in significant amounts of money and life savings it is best to spend some time pondering and then arriving at a decision instead of being carried away.

Ultimately all things in the long term whether stock market or real estate would rise because there is inflation and growth. The question however is how to maximize your return and get bang for your buck.

Sometimes holding on and waiting for dips could help you to do some great impact investing. Finally going forward do not always bet real estate would only go up. In short term it could dip. These present significant opportunities for value investing.

A **Warren Buffett** said about stock investing,

"I fear when others are greedy
and am
greedy when others are fearful."

Chapter 7

WHEN IS IT A BUBBLE IN THE STOCK MARKET?

How to recognise an over-heated market and avoid investing when the markets are ahead of fundamentals

---

"But a pin lies in wait for every bubble.
And when the two eventually meet, a new wave of investors learn some very old lessons: First, many in Wall Street — a community in which quality control is not prized — will sell investors anything they will buy.
Second, speculation is most dangerous
when it looks easiest."

– Warren Buffett

"Men, it has been well said, think in herds;
it will be seen that they go mad in herds,
while they only recover their senses slowly,
and
one by one."

– Charles Mackay

It was the 10th of March 2000 and the *NASDAQ* was at its peak at nearly 5048 nearly double the value just a year back. Harry sat back and relaxed in his chair at his desk and checked his portfolio of stocks. They had risen to mighty highs.

He sat there dreaming of quitting his job and going on that vacation he had longed for. Turks and Caicos or maybe Rio de Janeiro, he was still undecided. He was also thinking of changing his car. How about a new Mustang convertible? His mind was drifting away into infinite possibilities.

For over 5 years from 1995 on, the bubble had been forming; it was fed by cheap money and over-speculation. Fundamentals anyone? Who cared? It was a frenzy. Companies yet to generate revenue went public.

Some didn't even have finished products, but no one wanted to miss out. It was as you guessed it, the 'fear of missing out' - FOMO. IPOs (Initial Public Offerings) flew thick and fast hitting the market with great frequency and ferocity.

Buzz words like customised web-experience, internet, networking, virtual-malls kept the investors hooked and hungry for more.

Stock prices tripled and quadrupled on day one of listing. This was a new paradigm and new a tectonic shift that would change the lives of millions and stake billions. Big ideas were more important than solid business plans.

The commercialisation of the internet was the biggest opportunity to hit mankind in a long time and no one was going to miss that. It was a case of too much, too fast. In the year 1999, there were 457 IPOs most of which were technology and web related. Over a fourth of them doubled in price on the first day of listing. By 2001 the IPOs dwindled to 76.

As Harry dreamt on, just weeks later the dotcoms with hundreds of millions in market capitalization came crumbling down, just like castles and dreams built on thin air collapse.

Soon by the end of the year, majority of these dotcom companies folded and trillions of dollars of capital just evaporated. Young twenty something Silicon-Valley multi-millionaires were forced to move out from their multi-million-dollar estates and had to move back with their parents.

Harry's dream vacation and new car evaporated with the bust. Harry pulled up early at his office parking lot; he was worried about keeping his job which was hanging by a single thread. All dreams imploded spectacularly as people scrambled to get their lives back to normal. The frenzy had ended in a bubble burst.

The Red Indian and the Weather-man

The story of the Red Indian and the Weather-man in this context is an apt analogy. Once one autumn, the Red Indians asked their newly elected Chief if the coming winter was going to be severe or mild.

The Chief was a man of the modern era and could not really predict how severe the winter would turn out. Nevertheless, to be on the safer side he told his tribe that the coming winter was likely to be cold and that they should start collecting firewood.

This modern Chief felt that he needed to be on the safe side for his tribe who were dependent on his words. Thus, a week later, he quietly went to the phone booth and called the National Weather Service to confirm his predictions. They confirmed that the winter was indeed going to be a cold one.

Armed with this information, the Chief asked his tribe to collect more firewood for the winter. A fortnight later, the Chief again called in the National Weather Services and asked "Is it truly going to be a severely cold winter?", "Oh yes, extremely severe" they said confirming his suspicions.

This spurred the Chief and reiterated his beliefs. He warned his tribe of the coming of a harsh and prolonged winter, and urged them to collect every bit of firewood they could find.

Just in case, a week later, the Chief again called the National Weather Service and repeated the question. He asked, "Are you totally sure that the winter is going to be very cold and severe?" The weatherman replied, "Yes, we are certain that it's going to be one of history's worst winters". "How can you be so certain?" the chief asked. "The Red Indians are desperately collecting every scrap of wood, that's why!!" came quick the reply.

That is how the stock market could function. They could feed on themselves and in the process build a bubble.

Enduring Qualities of a Good Investor

One of the important aspects about being a good investor is the ability to recognise when to take a step back from investing and avoid the euphoria of rising stock markets. As **Benjamin Graham** said years ago,

"Price is what you Pay
and
Value is what you Get".

It would be smart and wise to avoid buying stocks when prices are high and the value is hard to find. Why is such a simple concept difficult to follow? The answer is human emotion.

We tend to be greedy when circumstances are euphoric and fearful when the situation turns gloomy. Investors tend to be swept by the tide of popular sentiment rather than thinking for themselves and having a balanced approach.

In the words of **Warren Buffett**;

"The most important quality for an investor
is temperament, not intellect."

When is the rise in the Stock Market justified?

Equity prices or stock prices reflect the expectations of the future stream in earnings. The expectations of future stream in earnings, in turn depend on the expectations of the future economic activity.

From the investor's point of view the most dominant predictor of sustainable increase in the value of equities or stocks in the stock market is the growth in GDP. A good GDP growth rate always points to rising and healthy stock markets.

One would be comfortable with a rising stock market when the GDP of the country is growing healthily. This rise in the market has to be tempered, as a rapid rise usually provides the impetus for elated investment.

This is why one should not get carried away with rapid rise in prices.

Why are Bubbles Formed?

"Only when the tide goes out
do you discover
Who's been swimming naked."

- *Warren Buffett*

"We will have another bubble, but usually
you don't get it the same way
as you got it before."

- *Warren Buffett*

The valuation of any stock is based on its earnings and the future growth potential of its earnings. Since the potential future growth in its earnings cannot be ascertained, there is always some speculation. Normally, when there is a stream of factors doing well in the economy, such as lower inflation, growth in GDP, increased exports, low unemployment figures etc., they make the market and economy look up.

Sometimes the rising markets feed on the stream of good news and everything begins to rise. After a point, the rest of the market that was not part of the rise join the bandwagon and they are consumed by the euphoria of growth which spirals further and further, well ahead of the fundamentals and beyond the boundaries of justification.

It is then that the market gets overheated and begins to enter bubble territory. There would be wide-spread justification by analysts telling us why this time things are different.

Yet, at this point, the lessons learnt from history and past trends about the market seem distant and are part of the blurred and forgotten past. The market is churning and moving ahead quickly, feeding on itself, as it marches along and builds castles in thin air.

At this point even highly intelligent people and people who have been saying all along that the market is overpriced, often get swept up in the storm of optimism for the fear of missing out. It would take great discipline to not be tempted by the rising markets. The only thing that can be said is, in Warren Buffett's words

"For Every Bubble A Pin Awaits"

When the music stops the person holding the parcel will pay a heavy price and then when the bubble bursts sanity is reclaimed. Hence being calm and keeping one's head during such times requires discipline and smartness that would make one a great investor.

It is always important to remember that the fundamentals of a stock or the stock market always prevails no matter what highs the euphoria and fervour bring. Hence investing according to fundamentals most often makes for good and successful investments.

The 'Warren Buffett Indicator'

"What we learn from history is that
people don't learn from history."

- *Warren Buffett*

"When the map and the territory don't agree,
always believe the territory."

- *Gause and Weinberg,*
(*Swedish Army Training*)

How could we quantify and assess if the stock market is in bubble space? The idea is to use the 'Buffett Indicator'. In a December 2001 article for *Fortune Magazine*, market guru, Warren Buffett, described this ratio as:

"(Warren Buffett Indicator is)
The best single measure of where valuations stand at any given moment."

The 'Buffett Indicator' is the total market capitalization of U.S. stocks relative to the GDP of the country.

In the same article in the *Fortune Magazine* back in 2001, Warren Buffett indicated that when the value of all stocks is 80% or less than the size of the economy, "buying stocks is likely to work very well for you". A value above 100 per cent is considered risky, while a figure above 120 per cent signals a bubble territory.

It is also to be noted that the GNP measure can be used in place of the GDP measure. GDP measures all economic activity within the nation's borders, even if that output is generated by foreign citizens or companies. GNP, on the other hand, focuses on the output of all the national companies, even if they are generating that economic activity outside the country.

The 'Warren Buffett' Indicator is a clear indicator of when to sit on cash and when to deploy. When too high and above 120% we know we are in bubble territory and we would do well to step back from the market. Anything above 100% and we are in the overheated territory. Anything below 80% and the situation is favourable to buy more of equities.

More than just a stand-alone metric, it is best used when it is compared to itself at different points in time. This would tell us how attractive the stock market is to invest during those points in time. We could increase or decrease our exposure based on this metric.

If the charts on the stock market (the map) do not agree with what you see, in comparison to the 'Buffett Indicator' (the territory), believe in the 'Buffett indicator' (the territory), because it tracks where you actually are rather than the charts. So, the next time you invest in stocks keep the 'Warren Buffett' indicator in mind.

Does this indicator work for developing countries like INDIA?

In developing countries like INDIA, a significant part of the economy may not be formalised or maybe unlisted. INDIA is home to a large informal sector, consisting of millions of individual businesses, small and medium enterprises. Though small in size, together they contribute to a significant part of the country's output and create employment in the economy.

Apart from these there are a number of privately held enterprises in INDIA which are highly successful, which choose not to list because of either compliance issues or because they prefer to raise private capital.

Hence, most of the businesses operating in economies in countries like INDIA may not be listed.

So probably a good measure to use, for developing countries like INDIA, would be the 'aggregate P/E' ratio, which tells us the total price of all stocks in the market divided by all the aggregate earnings. If we do a historical time series this would give us a good indication of whether the market is overpriced or undervalued.

Now, though when directly applied the 'Buffett indicator' is not the best measure for a developing country like INDIA, it could still serve as a supporting measure.

It could be compared relatively, against itself in a time series over a period of time. It could serve as a guide, helping us to either increase or decrease exposure to the stock market, according to whether the market is undervalued or overheated respectively.

Conclusion

It is important for any investor to know whether s/he is putting money into a market at value, under value or if the market is overheated. Investors are more likely to burn their fingers when they invest in the market when it is over-heated.

No matter the temporary gloom or euphoria in the market, reflected in the prices, one should always track the fundamentals to make informed investment decisions.

The 'Buffett Indicator' or the 'aggregate P/E' indicators are simple and practical guides to follow when one invests in the market. So, use these indicators to guide you through your investments and in the market.

Chapter 8

USEFUL ECONOMICS FOR ADMINISTRATORS

Some 'basic knowledge' of economics will go a long way with helping one deal with the Stock and Bond markets

---

"Economics is not an exact science.
"First rule of Economics 101:
Our desires are insatiable.
Second rule:
We can stomach only three Big Macs at a time."

- Douglas Horton

It's a combination of an art
and
elements of science.
And that's almost the first and last lesson to be learned about economics:
that in my judgment, we are not converging toward exactitude,
but we're improving our data bases and our ways of reasoning about them."

- Paul Samuelson

FISCAL DEFICIT

Fiscal deficit is the difference between the government expenditure and the net taxes raised. Often government expenditure exceeds net taxes.

When the total expenses made by the government exceeds its' revenues (excluding its borrowings) it is known as "Fiscal Deficit". When the government needs to spend and is short of funds, the funds could potentially be raised by three methods.

The government could:

- Raise Taxes,
- Issue Government Bonds or
- Print Money

When the government issues bonds, it would compete with the private sector for public savings. If the government's requirement is large, it would 'crowd out' the ability of the private sector to raise money.

Lastly, the government could also dip into capital inflows from the rest of the world.

Understanding what 'Fiscal Deficit' is as important for a bond investor as it is for a stock investor. A large 'Fiscal Deficit' could lead to a rise in market interest rates and drop in bond prices. On the contrary, when 'Fiscal Deficit' is under control it is good for the bond prices.

Similarly, large 'Fiscal Deficits' could mean higher interest rates and the lowering of private borrowing and investments, which in turn could affect stock market growth, private sector growth and consequently private sector employment generation.

Huge 'Fiscal Deficit' may lead to higher taxes, which could slow down consumer spending and consequently business investment. On the contrary when 'Fiscal Deficit' is under control it could lead to lower taxes.

This would lead to higher consumer spending and higher corporate expenditure driving forward the economy.

Generally higher 'Fiscal Deficit' leads to:

- Higher levels of debt to GDP ratio leading to higher taxes. This would slow the economy and would serve as a disincentive to labour effort and entrepreneurial activity
- The government may have to print money to finance the deficit leading to higher inflation.
- The **'Crowding out'** of private investment as the government corners all the savings in the economy to fund the deficit.

Some of the FISCAL POLICY TOOLS available at the disposal of the government:

- **Current Government Spending:**

  Current government spending, such as spending on goods and services, health, education, and defence also add to the government expenditure and impacts the country's overall productivity, skill and security, and plays a role in the country's development.

- **Capital Expenditure:**

  Capital expenditure such as spending on infrastructure, roads, hospitals, schools etc., also, increases the 'Fiscal Deficit'.

  Yet, such expenditure also helps to improve the country's capital stock and in turn strengthens the productivity of the economy.

- **Indirect Taxes:**

  Taxes levied on a variety of goods and services including manufactured products, fuel and services are indirect taxes. They are also referred to as sales tax, value added tax (VAT) or goods and services tax (GST) etc.

  Taxes are levied to raise revenues to finance expenditure on infrastructure, hospitals, medical care, bridging social inequalities, facilitating commerce and encouraging good behaviour, which are for the benefit of the citizens.

- **Direct Taxes:**

  Taxes levied on income and wealth on a personal level, and on corporate profits at a corporate level, help in direct tax collection. Other taxes such as capital gains tax, social security tax and inheritance tax also come under direct taxes.

All of them help in wealth re-distribution and also help increase the revenue collection for the government and in the reduction of the 'Fiscal Deficit'.

- **Transfer of Payments:**

  While welfare payments made through social security system comprising of state pensions, housing benefits, income support, child benefits, unemployment benefits, job search allowances etc., help to address the inequality in society they contribute to the rise in the 'Fiscal Deficit'.

Overall, from an investment point of view, it is necessary for one to understand what is 'Fiscal Deficit' and what are the tools in the hands of the government to deal with it.

When we do understand these concepts and the tools that are in the hands of the government, we would also learn to gauge the effects of government decisions on the economy.

Moreover, this would also help us evaluate its effects on industry and thus our investments. With the basic knowledge and understanding of fiscal policy, we could make informed investment decisions.

MONETARY POLICY

While it's the government that decides the 'Fiscal Policy', it is the nation's central bank or federal bank that decides the country's 'Monetary Policy'.

'Monetary Policy' guides the course of action taken by the nation's central bank to change the target interest rate, reserve requirements and changes in bank reserve. This affects the aggregate output and prices in the economy and can be used as tools to either speed up a slowing economy or prevent overheating of the economy by reining it in.

Most countries follow a 'Fractional Banking' system in which each bank must hold reserves at least equal to the reserve ratio times its customer deposits. Any excess cash can be lent to other banks that need reserves to meet their reserve requirements.

Central banks can increase the money supply in the economy by buying securities from banks, lowering of reserve ratio or targeting the interest rates at which banks borrow and lend to each other. When money supply is increased in the economy it normally causes lowering of lending rates and spurs the economy. This is a tool used by the central bank to spur a slowing economy.

When a central bank buys securities, it does so by paying for them, thus increasing the money supply in the economy. This tends to spur the economy further. The Central bank can also decrease the cash reserve ratio. Reducing the cash reserve ratio has a similar effect where it increases the amount of deposits a bank can take while maintaining the reserves the banks are mandated to hold.

Thirdly the Central bank could target the interbank lending rates. If it raises the rate, it will slow the economy, by decreasing the money supply, while cutting the rates spurs the economy and increases the money supply.

The actions of the central bank can have a direct impact on the stock and bond markets. If there is a decrease in interest rates due to central bank actions, it makes lending cheaper, spurs the economy and the future expectations of the stock market.

Similarly, the cutting of rates causes the bond market to rally as bondholders benefit from higher rates they had previously locked in.

On the flip side, the increase in rates, negatively impacts the bond market. The stock markets are positively impacted when market interest rates are cut. The state of the economy often necessitates corrective actions by the central bank to keep the economy of the country on an even keel.

The Effect of 'FISCAL' and 'MONETARY' Policies

Analysts focus on the 'Fiscal Deficit' to understand the government's intention and plan for the economy.

If the 'Fiscal Deficit' is large and continues to grow by the year, it is assumed that the government is following a loose or expansionary fiscal policy.

The opposite is when the government is pruning the 'Fiscal Deficit' at which times a contractionary fiscal policy is said to be adopted.

Normally, if the economy slows and the unemployment rises, the government's spending on unemployment benefits and public investments for employment generation, infrastructure spending, would increase to add to the aggregate demand.

The government normally resorts to an expansionary policy to spur the economy and increase employment.

Similarly, if there is a boom, it increases employment and profits, it causes increases in tax collection and there is a decrease in deficit (or sometimes a surplus). If the government spending and revenues are equal then the budget is balanced.

Although both fiscal and monetary policy can alter aggregate demand they do so through different channels and have differing impacts.

The two policies are not interchangeable. Consider the following cases in which the assumption is made that *wages and prices are rigid*:

An EXPANSIONARY Fiscal Policy/TIGHT Monetary Policy:

If an expansionary policy is followed by the government where government spending rises and the taxes are cut it would lead to an increase in aggregate demand and spur the economy.

However, a tight monetary policy will offset the fiscal expansion, as increase in rates will dampen the private sector even as the public sector flourishes.

Here government spending will be a larger part of the country's GDP.

A CONTRACTIONARY Fiscal Policy/EASY Monetary Policy:

If the government follows a contractionary fiscal policy reigning in government spending and raising taxes and this is accompanied by an easy monetary policy, where the interest rates are lowered, then the private sector will expand handsomely and would have a larger share of the GDP output than the public sector.

An EXPANSIONARY Fiscal Policy/EASY Monetary Policy:

If both the fiscal and monetary policies are easy, then the joint impact will be highly expansionary growing both the public and private sectors.

A CONTRACTIONARY Fiscal Policy/TIGHT Monetary Policy:

If both the fiscal and monetary policies are played tight, it would lead to a drop in aggregate demand slowing down the economy and slowing both the private and public sectors of the economy.

LEADING and LAGGING Economic Indicators

Some of the useful economic indicators that show the direction of the economy are the 'Lead', 'Lag' and 'Coincident' indicators. They usually have value in predicting the near-term future state of the economy.

While the 'Lead' indicators have turning points that usually precede the overall direction of the economy, the 'Lag' indicators have turning points that occur later than those of the overall economy.

The 'Coincident' indicators on the other hand have turning points that coincide with the direction of the economy.

While the 'Lead' indicators help to predict the future direction of the economy, the 'Lag' indicators help us to understand the past. In the US, the composite leading indicator is called the (LEI) the index of the Leading Economic Indicators and it has ten components.

It is useful to be aware of these indicators as they point to the overall future direction of the economy and the health of the stock markets correspondingly.

However, the combination of this index does vary from country to country.

In the US for instance the composition of the Leading indicators includes:

Sn.	Leading Indicator	Explanation
1.	Average weekly hours, manufacturing	This is a leading indicator because businesses will cut overtime before laying off workers in a downturn and the opposite holds true when the economy is up and businesses pay overtime before hiring.
2.	Average weekly initial claims for unemployment insurance	This is an indicator of layoffs and unemployment
3.	Manufacturers' new orders for consumer goods and materials	This captures the upturn in the economy with the initial order of manufacturers' goods and material to be used to service their consumers before the products hit the market.
4.	Vendor performance, slower deliveries diffusion index	This signals the sentiment and demand unfolding in the economy as orders are delivered quickly.
5.	Manufacturers' new orders for non-defence capital goods	When manufacturers order new capital equipment it is a sign that they are preparing for demand in the economy and an upturn.
6.	Building permits for new private housing units	This indicator foretells the uptick in future construction activity.
7.	S&P 500 Stock Index	S&P broadly anticipates an upturn in the economy and is a good indicator of the future health of the economy.
8.	Money supply, real M^2	Increases in money supply would mean businesses can borrow at lower rates and is a good indicator of possible upward shift in the economy.
9.	Interest rate spread between 10-year treasury yields and overnight borrowing rates	When the interest rate spread is large and it is in anticipation of an upswing as one expects more demand for money and an economic up-cycle.
10.	Index of Consumer Expectations	It is an insight into future consumer spending and the possibility of the economic health of the country looking bright.

(Source: Understanding Business Cycles, by Michele Gambera, PhD, CFA, Milton Ezrati, and Bolong Cao, PhD, CFA)

Balance of Trade Deficit

A 'Balance of Trade Deficit' occurs when the domestic economy is spending more on foreign services and goods than what foreign economies are spending on one's domestic goods and services.

It can also imply that the country is spending more than it produces because the domestic savings are not enough to finance domestic spending plus the government fiscal balance.

The country could fund this deficit by borrowing from the rest of the world through the financial markets. The rest of the world may be able to provide this fund because it correspondingly must be running a trade surplus and spending less than it produces.

In other words, one's deficit may be another's surplus and the trade and capital flows between economies are always in balance.

However, it is to be noted that though foreign countries may help to bridge the gap, the terms of financing or trade may or not be favourable to the domestic economy.

The Significance of the 'Yield Curve'

When we take bonds of comparable credit quality but differing maturity dates and plot its interest rates at a set point in time we get a yield curve.

Most commonly the treasury debt plotted over a 3 month, 2-yr, 5-yr or 30-yr period is reported which forms a bench mark for other debt in the market such as mortgage rates and bank lending rates.

The 'Yield Curve' is most importantly used to predict economic output and growth in the economy.

The shape of the yield curve gives us an indication of the future direction of interest rates and hence economic activity.

There are 3 KINDS of **YIELD CURVES:**

- Normal
- Inverted
- Flat (or humped)

Normal Yield Curve:

A 'Normal Yield Curve' is upward sloping where the longer-term maturity bonds have higher yields than short term maturity bonds because of the risks associated with time. A 'Normal Yield Curve' is often associated with **economic expansion.**

When the expected demand for money in the future is going to be good, and the interest rates are also moving higher, these signs indicate that the economy will do well and is going to expand.

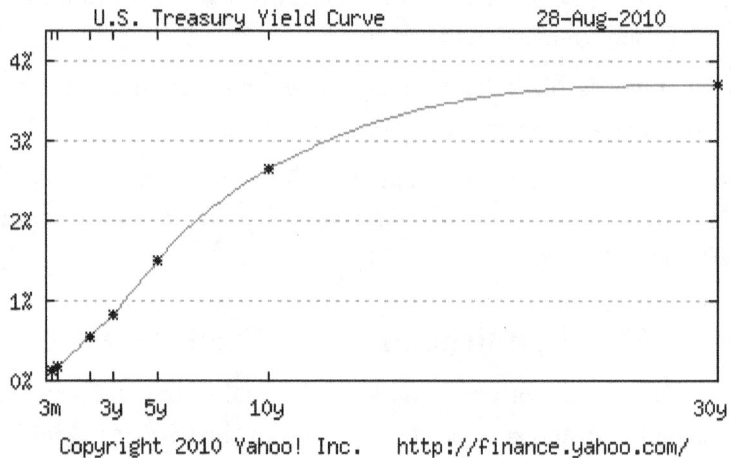

Inverted Yield Curve:

An 'Inverted Yield Curve' is one in which short term maturity bonds have a higher yield than long term maturity bonds. Importantly an **'Inverted Yield Curve'** is a **sign of an impending recession.**

In an impending recession the market would anticipate less demand for money by the economy in the future and therefore lower interest rates in the future.

When investors believe that the interest rates of bonds in the future would be lower they would try and lock in long term bonds pushing up their demand but decreasing their yields in the process. Hence, we would have an inverted structure.

Flat Yield Curve:

A 'Flat Yield Curve' is one in which the shorter- and longer-term yields are at similar levels. It is a predictor of economic transition.

A 'Yield Curve' is a handy predictor of the course of an economy. Additionally, particular note needs to be on the **inverted yield curve as it may be the sign of an impending recession**.

Conclusion

While this chapter is not meant to be a lesson in economics, it does highlight some important concepts that would come in handy for investors to study and to make investment decisions in the stock market, bond market or real estate market.

Hence, any fresh investor seeking to make their first investment decision would be greatly benefitted when they are introduced to the existence and utility of these concepts.

The information would help one to digest and also better understand the news on the economy and the news in the media, to make better and more informed decisions with respect to investing.

Do learn more about these and incorporate these in your analysis when you invest. They provide useful cues to the health and direction of the economy.

Chapter 9

BALANCE OF WORLD POWERS

How there are going to be dramatic shifts in the balance of world power this century

---

"He who has great power should use it lightly."

- *Lucius Annaeus Seneca*

"Our great power
does not mean
we can do whatever we want whenever we want,
nor
should we assume
we have all the wisdom and knowledge necessary to succeed."

- *John McCain*

Before we try to understand the shifts in world power that this century would bring, we need to understand what we mean by world power.

World power has three major dimensions. These are 'economic power', 'military power' and then there is 'soft power'.

It is expected that in the current century, the world powers would rebalance themselves and there would be a shift in the centers of power with the rise of new players.

The Asian Century

*"Before we acquire great power,
we must acquire
wisdom to use it well."*

- *Ralph Waldo Emerson*

*"Leadership is about vision and responsibility,
not power."*

- *Seth Berkley*

This century would see a reset at the table where world powers meet and discuss. It may not be known to many people that for thousands of years until late 1700s, the centre of world power, its *GDP* and soft power lay in Asia, with the two Asian giants, namely China and India. Together, they constituted more than 60% of the world's GDP.

They were also the power centres of education, culture and the arts. From the late 1700s however, over the next 250 years, there was a decline in their shares of GDP and world power, to the point that they became marginal players.

Europe and then America rose through rapid industrialisation, while Asia stood exploited for resources that rapidly dwindled as the Europeans took over the world.

However, this century, China and India have begun to play catch up in turbo mode. China with a head start on reforms has shed its communist leanings to embrace capitalism and has risen phenomenally over the last 4 decades. India is 15 years behind China and has begun to pull up its socks.

It has transformed its mixed economy with economic liberalization and market reform. It is expected that by mid-century China, India and United States would be the three largest economies in the world. The shift of the economic power centre to Asia would be complete.

Beyond China and India there are more, well, surprises. Indonesia could become the fourth largest economy in the world while Mexico and Turkey could grow bigger than Germany and France.

Other rising powers include Saudi Arabia, Nigeria, Egypt, Pakistan, Iran, Philippines and Vietnam. All of these nations would rank higher and would be larger economies than Italy and other smaller European nations.

Since the end of World War II, the US has been a dominant player in the international system and was central in creating new international organisations such as the United Nations, NATO, IMF and the World Bank. American diplomacy spearheaded agreements on trade, climate change, arms control and it also assured regional and world security.

Americans were always at the forefront formulating and directing the "rule based international order" and they stood by guaranteeing the same. Moreover, the United States of America took it upon itself to maintain a level of sanctity with respect to international agreements and order.

Since 2016, the US has upheld a more introspective policy under its new President and has also slowly begun to withdraw from its international engagements. This has left a vacuum. Russia and more so China, have begun to fill this vacuum and these nations have become more assertive and visible.

It is not just these two major powers but as America's global role has been diminishing, a growing number of countries have begun asserting their independent views and these countries are taking up influential roles in the regional and economic playbooks of their neighbourhood.

However, having made these observations, it is not that Asia's rise is inevitable. If the drivers that are fuelling their rise could falter, their rise in power and domination could also deflate. China could for instance, go into a political meltdown, similar to its last great empire.

The Indian economy may face problems from the *Naxal* unrest, communal problems peppered with caste-based friction and uprising. Japan may continue to shrink with its ageing population.

However, barring any such setback, Asia will see an inevitable rise and the shift of power from west to east is bound to happen.

Economic Power

"Power is like being a lady...
if you have to tell people you are,
you aren't."

- *Margaret Thatcher*

"Power is the great aphrodisiac."

- *Henry Kissinger*

By 2050, the three largest economies in the world would be China, India and United States. China as of 2019 had already overtaken the United States with a higher *GDP (Gross Domestic Product)* in terms of *PPP (Purchasing Power Parity)*.

It is estimated that by the year 2030 India would overtake the United States and become the second largest economy in PPP terms.

These projections may surprise many who have been blind-sided by the rapid development of China and by those who have viewed India as a backwater in the past.

However, this would not come as a surprise to those who have been following these two nations closely. It is only to be expected that with their large populations these nations would achieve higher GDPs.

GDP is a product of Labour, Capital and *'Total factor productivity'* or *TFP*. Given that these nations are endowed with large number of human resources, even with a small injection of capital, local or foreign, these nations could realise their potential in a short period of time.

The TFP which represents the contribution of innovation and technology to the GDP would also accelerate the rise of China and India. With respect to the growth of GDP, other countries like Indonesia, Brazil and Turkey are also likely to figure in the Top 10 nations by the year 2050.

The rise of these nations would cause huge shifts in world trade and lead to the formation of new trading partnerships and blocs.

This would lead to a new world order as economic power would facilitate military power, influence and reach. A multi polar world with new power centres would be created.

It needs to be seen if this change and replacement of the old-world order with a new one, leads to more prosperity or conflict in the future.

The world would hope for the peaceful rise of nations, especially China.

As **Seneca** had wisely said,

"He who has great power
should use it lightly."

Military Power

"I hope our wisdom will grow with our power,
and teach us, that
the less we use our power
the greater it will be."

- Thomas Jefferson

"A great power has to have the discipline
not only to go when necessary but to know when not to go.
Getting involved in ethnic, religious civil wars is a recipe for disaster."

- John Kasich

While the economic rise of China and India is inevitable, the United States, in the early part of this century, would still dominate the world in terms of its military power. However, as China is focussed on becoming a world power, it would provide a stiff challenge to the US and assert its position wherever and whenever possible.

It is also to be understood that the huge influence of the US military-industrial complex creates undue influence on US foreign policy and distorts it. It sometimes forces the United States to act in ways which are detrimental to it in the long term, which detracts from its moral authority.

An example of this is the war to oust Saddam Hussein based on questionable evidence of *WMDs (Weapons of Mass Destruction)* which were actually never found. Military force has often been the most preferred choice and has been higher up in the deck of cards that the US wishes to play.

It has mostly marginalised diplomacy and other instruments that would have won it more legitimacy and world support. The Trump Presidency has been inward looking, the US military has grown while its diplomatic force has shrunk further, thus fuelling this failing approach. The old adage that rings true in this context.

"If the only tool you have
is a hammer,
then every problem becomes a nail."

China has made its entrance as a formidable power. This along with its new assertiveness and the fading legitimacy of the United States has led nations under the security guarantee of the United States to ponder.

It is expected that these nations that are dependent on the United States for their security would need to strengthen their own military and take matters into their own hands.

This would create a multipolar world with a number of power centres trying to jostle and outdo one another. In other words, we are entering an uncertain era where new powers and new power alignments would begin to act independently, which may add to the disorderliness of the world affairs. The 'power vacuums' left by the US are likely to be filled by China and others.

With its economic clout, China is likely to snare a number of smaller countries into its net with projects such as the now infamous 'lend-indebt-snare' strategy. This helps the 'Old Imperial Nation' to buy the ability to form military bases through influence strategies and also establish points of influence to project power around the world.

It is also possible that if China does not rise peacefully, a war with one or the other major military power would be inevitable.

While in the new future, China may not be able to match the United States militarily, no one should underestimate the resolve of the Chinese Communist leadership that seeks to get China back to its glorious past. China blinded by past humiliations and with the pride of its magnificent past could be a military threat to a number of other nations.

In this century, the United States and China are likely to jostle, push and shove as the United States begins to accommodate the rise of China.

Not for nothing does China call itself the 'Middle kingdom'. It truly considers itself the 'Centre of the world' and an indispensable world power.

Soft Power

"Power is of two kinds.
One is obtained by the fear of punishment
and the other
by acts of love.
Power based on love is a thousand times more effective and permanent than the one derived from fear of punishment."

- Mahatma Gandhi

"We thought,
because we had power, we had wisdom."

- Stephen Vincent Benet

Hu Shih, the Chinese philosopher and diplomat once said "India conquered and dominated China culturally for 20 centuries without ever having to send a single soldier across her border".

This just highlights that no country really needs to dominate another militarily or economically. It is possible to be an influential soft power without the need to coerce or bribe.

'Power' is the ability to obtain outcomes one would desire. This can be accomplished by 'carrots' using one's economic power, through 'sticks' using one's military power or by using the powers of persuasion and one's attraction.

While the former two are components of hard power the last is what soft power is all about. It is the ability to obtain favourable outcomes without payment or use of force.

Rather than thinking of soft power as power over others, one should look at it as power to accomplish anything by taking others along with you. The power of persuasion that convinces and influences many to move along with you is a vital asset and this is what soft power can accomplish.

In the last century, Great Britain and the United States wielded their soft power to great effect by being the centre of the global movie and music industries. Along with the advantage of the English language, power over the media, the cultural appeal of liberty and their philosophies about freedom, they have been able to fuel dreams which have consequent influence and charm.

The early success of capitalism along with the promise of the life of freedom and liberty had its magical effects which even led to the demise of the once powerful U.S.S.R. The United States overcame the U.S.S.R through the appeal and the benefits of capitalism, with its subtle projection of the good life, promise of liberty and life with freedom.

Such is the power of 'Soft-power'. In the age of media and the power of its other forms such as social media, nations can be appealing because of their soft power and thus they need not necessarily wield the stick or carrot to have their way.

Conclusion

"The attempt to combine wisdom and power has only rarely been successful and then only for a short while."

- Albert Einstein

"What it lies in our power to do, it lies in our power not to do."

- Aristotle

"It is certain, in any case, that ignorance, allied with power, is the most ferocious enemy justice can have."

- James Baldwin

A nation's ability to combine the three powers described namely, determines its true power.

- Economic Power,
- Military Power (and)
- Soft Power

Sometimes empowering others helps us to attain common goals. The efficacy of the nation to achieve a successful strategy, hinges on its ability to combine these three dimensions of power seamlessly.

At the very foundation of soft power is the subtle appeal of a nation's popular culture and its ability to connect with nations and their people across the world.

While 'Soft power' alone may not be able to solve many problems, its influence should not be underestimated.

Broad acceptance and ability to forge common ground would be needed among nations to accomplish many of the goals to make this world a better place for everyone.

Let us hope that common sense would prevail and more world powers use persuasion and soft power rather than forcing their way with their economic and military might.

Chapter 10

THE FUTURE OF CONFLICT

God forbid and hope that better sense prevails

"I know not with what weapons World War III will be fought,
but World War IV will be fought with
sticks and stones."

- *Albert Einstein*

"The tragedy of modern war is that the young men die
fighting each other - instead of their real enemies
back home in the capitals."

- *Edward Abbey*

The future of conflict is not easy to visualize because it takes unexpected routes and opens new dimensions that have not been thought of before. Although one thing is certain, one would be naïve to believe there would be no conflict.

War in the past has been fought for conquests, resources, religion and even for a single woman. It only needs a small reason to get the testosterone of men flowing. Warriors of the past are glorified or vilified to romanticize war; lo and behold the drums of war begin to beat.

Hitler, Genghis Khan, and Alexander have more pages written about them in history books than Mahatma Gandhi. This in itself gives you a good prognosis of what the future holds. We will always have humans waging war with one another despite however stupid it may seem.

Mistrust, greed, hate, and power have incited humans into fights over and over again. To expect that this would somehow end would make one callow. Yet to expect that this could be contained is more pragmatic.

We hope that in the future wars can be few and far between, and the world would be largely peaceful for our children to thrive without fear and with freedom.

History of War

"Anyone who has ever looked into the glazed eyes of a soldier dying on the battlefield
will think hard
before starting a war."

- *Otto von Bismarck*

"The real trouble with war (modern war) is that it gives
no one a chance to kill the right people."

- *Ezra Pound*

"Hollywood never knew there was a Vietnam War
until
they made the movie."

- *Jerry Stiller*

Wars have been part of human existence from the earliest of times when humans began to fight over food, women, property, resources, and land.

While there was a time when battles were fought person to person, gun to gun, tank to tank and plane to plane, in the coming years most war would be waged by unknown faces sitting behind computers and fighting via keyboards and servers over the world-wide-web with digital and autonomous weapons.

Combat between humans was first in close quarters. Initially, physical combat that involved body contact, wrestling, fighting using swords, sticks, and stones. Slowly the art of war developed and the distance between the combatants grew.

Man progressed to more advanced weapons and greater skill with archery, slingshots, and catapults that meant that one could kill from a distance. The coming of guns allowed for killing from an even greater distance.

This was followed by long-distance rifles, cannons, and machine guns. With the invention of propeller airplanes, jet aircraft, frigates, aircraft carriers and finally long-range missiles, humans were able to strike from land, sea, and air. With cruise missiles, militaries were able to strike from over vast distances.

With the coming of Intercontinental ballistic missiles, no part of the world was safe. Now war has been taken into space and the weaponization of space has started with new laser, electromagnetic and microwave weapons.

While nations strategize to suffer minimum damage and costs to themselves, cyber warfare, irregular, unconventional and asymmetric warfare have begun to take centre stage as the preferred methods for undermining the enemy.

With rapid progress in AI (Artificial Intelligence) a new dimension to warfare has been added, making it more deadly and impersonal, and consequently more inhuman.

Autonomous Machines and AI (Artificial Intelligence)

"You can't say civilization don't advance...
in every war,
they kill you in a new way."

- *Will Rogers*

"In war, you win or lose, live or die –
and the difference
is just an eyelash."

- *Douglas MacArthur*

Autonomous fighting machines have the ability to identify and neutralize enemy combatants and targets without human intervention.

This is complicated because once unleashed these machines do not need an authorization for every strike. This opens up new dimensions and dilemmas in their command-and-control systems. Humans can often take complex decisions on the battlefield which machines may not.

While AI-enabled machines have to be trained for different scenarios, it may not be possible to train AI for every complex eventuality. Ultimately, these systems are not going to be easy to build.

Generals understand how situations change in micro-seconds. They need to take cognisance of many aspects such as on-ground situations, enemy strategies/weaknesses and of course international relations. Hence, they certainly do not want to hand over authority to machines to act without oversight.

However, we could expect such autonomous machines in the future. There are already autonomous sea-based drones that look for threats at sea and aerial autonomous drones that scan the horizons and the ground for enemy combatants.

We are unsure at this point whether these autonomous drones would be armed in the future and whether they will be allowed to strike down intruders and trespassers on their own. However, it is unlikely that they would be allowed to act on their own and take calculated autonomous decisions to destroy the enemies they identify without oversight.

The future of such weapons, have a lot of unknowns and it is to be seen how autonomous these autonomous vehicles would truly become.

Cyber-warfare

"Cyber-war takes place largely in secret,
unknown to the general public on both sides."

- *Noah Feldman*

"Developments in information technology and globalized media mean that the
most powerful military in the history of the world can lose a war,
not on the battlefield of dust and blood,
but on the battlefield of world opinion."

- *Timothy Garton Ash*

'Cyber-warfare' involves crippling the adversary by using computer systems and the internet in order to incapacitate or undermine the adversary. The most frightening thing about cyber-warfare is that it takes very little to start.

A large-scale devastating attack can be started by even a single motivated person or team. There would be no need for large scale investments or government approval. The threat is immediate and immense.

With our daily lives being more and more intertwined with digital systems any attack could disrupt our lives, career, needs and habits in a big way. It could put millions out of the resources they need to survive.

In the future, cyber-warfare would be conducted against the electrical power grid, water supply stations, financial, and military installations. These public utilities when controlled by smart tools and technologies become vulnerable to cyber-attacks and are hence capable of bringing down whole smart cities and could wreak havoc in day-to-day life itself. Additionally, when nuclear power plants become targets, the potential meltdown and disaster is incalculable.

Cyber-ware could sabotage satellites, critical information servers, modes of transportation, communication systems, and all of this could be done from halfway around the world.

The technologies for these forms of covert attacks are slowly developing and could soon become a stark reality.

The types of disruptions that are possible in the future include:

- **DDoS attacks**: In a DDoS or 'Distributed Denial of Service' attack could cut off resources that millions of people depend on and it could disrupt the lives of the entire population.
- **Ransomware**: Ransomware can be used to prevent system access. It could hold data at ransom until the user pays a specified ransom. This could be devastating if it hits critical infrastructure life services and hospitals. It could cost billions of dollars and cut off critical production and resources.
- **Bots**: Could be used to crack open sites by repeated attempts and could also help to penetrate vulnerabilities within systems
- **Injected Worms and Viruses**: Most systems can be incapacitated and made useless by attacks from worms and viruses. The systems can even be made to behave in undesirable ways or could be externally controlled.
- **IoT espionage**: IoT espionage can cause multiple level vulnerabilities where a large number of high-tech devices can be turned on to spy on the owner itself. This has huge security implications for a country as a whole.

Cyber-warfare includes the ability to take down military satellites, jam radar installations and disable infrared detection, lasers and all other kinds of future weapons.

Foreign adversaries could use viruses and backdoor switches to relay intelligence information on one's networks to themselves. They can also be used to destroy data and disenable servers at critical times.

Cyber-warfare, when combined with *EW* or *electronic-warfare*, has tremendous synergistic effects and these are complementary.

Here EW can be used to control the electromagnetic spectrum from which the enemy operates while cyber-warfare can be used to handicap and incapacitate the opponent by using their own networks against him.

With the era of AI (Artificial Intelligence) and computational neural networks upon us, new fronts for cyber-warfare will emerge. With the high levels of deniability in cyber-warfare, the perpetrators of cyber-crime could easily hide behind the curtain of anonymity.

Thus, this has now become the oft chosen tool to hassle and trouble adversaries.

Nuclear War

"In a nuclear war,
all men are cremated equal."

- *Dexter Gordon*

"The release of atomic energy has not created a new problem.
It has merely made more urgent
the necessity of solving
an
existing one."

- *Albert Einstein*

"Ours is a world of nuclear giants and ethical infants.
We know more about war
than
we know about peace,
more about killing
than
we know about living."

- *Omar N. Bradley*

Nuclear war may be unthinkable. Anyone who has seen the images of the unfortunate victims of the world's first and only (so far) atomic bomb targets that caused the devastation of Hiroshima and Nagasaki would know of its actual horrors. The effects have lasted over generations.

While the spread of nuclear weapons has been contained to a larger extent by world non-proliferation treaties, a handful of nations still continue to hold and develop these weapons. These states are unlikely to give them up soon.

The grim repercussions of nuclear war in Hiroshima and Nagasaki have been witnessed world over. Nuclear weapons have hence been so greatly demonized in the altar of world opinion that only a foolish country that has lost powers of its own nuclear armaments or one which faces an existential threat is likely to use them.

Nuclear weapons, ironically, because of their huge destructive nature have guaranteed peace by the doctrine of MAD (mutually assured destruction). Nuclear wars are unthinkable and cannot be won.

Nuclear weapons have become more of a status symbol and as a means of deterrence that helps to achieve military offensive objectives. The theatre of warfare has hence adapted to this new reality and we have other forms of warfare such as 'Asymmetric warfare' and 'Irregular warfare' which attain the objectives required more effectively.

While usage of nuclear weapons by rogue states and terrorist outfits are not ruled out in the future, those who use it will be at a complete loss of any sympathy from the rest of the world.

Hence, those who ever plan to use it will have to think many times over, as no civilized state would accept its usage in war or otherwise.

Economics of Warfare

"War is a racket.
It is the only one international in scope.
It is the only one in which
the profits are reckoned in dollars
and
the losses in lives."

- Smedley Butler

"War is the business
of
barbarians."

- Napoleon Bonaparte

"War:
a massacre of people who don't know each other
for the profit of people
who know each other
but
don't massacre each other."

- Paul Valery

"No army of the world can march on an empty stomach", these words attributed to Napolean Bonaparte, underline the economics of warfare. Anyone can start a war, but it is only a strong economy that can sustain it. Without a strong economy and logistical ability to back it, the war machine would come to a grinding halt.

Also, often wars are fought for economic reasons. The greed for resources drove the British, French, Dutch, Spaniards, Portuguese and other European powers to send their militaries to Africa and much of Asia.

The British conquered most of the earth and proclaimed that "the Sun never set on the British empire". The British often took the justification of "White man's burden" to justify its atrocities but the real reasons were obviously economic.

In recent times, commentators have purported that the United States started the Gulf-war to get a stranglehold of the oil in the middle-east. This is no surprise.

Throughout history, a number of the conflicts, even those which may have seemed to have had a religious spearhead, such as the crusades, are often nothing but thinly veiled attempts to get an upper hand for resources or economic power.

Religion was just a convenient vehicle to brainwash the gullible and shut down those who used their brains. Power and economics are the real reasons that motivate and charge the war machinery.

Given that most things in life are driven by economics, it is not surprising that wars are no different. When we actually take away the underlying economics, the real reasons for war would not be able to stand on their own feet.

There will always be leaders who will proclaim other reasons, but the underlying cause for wars are often just power and money.

Most people, for instance, are of the opinion that Pakistan is in a fight with India for Kashmir. They would say it is the religious background that keeps the fire lit. Most people in India and Pakistan would get fired up by their leaders, either on the fuse of patriotism, nationalism, religion, pride and hatred or survival instinct.

However, as ironical as it may seem, the real reason why Pakistan fights India and the reason told to the Pakistani public is different.

The Pakistan's public is told that India is an existential threat to Pakistan. Many people have been brainwashed to die in the name of religion or for "freedom", so that the generals of Pakistan and its army continue to be well funded to live luxurious lives.

The indifferent and callous decision to indoctrinate and send the young and naïve fighters across the border as jihadis, is a planned and motivated action by the generals and ISI (Inter-Services intelligence) of Pakistan.

This only serves to sustain the (Army and Intelligence) General's self-serving agenda. These Jihadis are brainwashed into believing that they would be rewarded in their after-life and as martyrs they would enter heaven, where seventy-two virgins were awaiting them.

All this is preached to impressionable minds to turn them into mere puppets that would do the general's bidding. While the youth are trained to take fanatic steps to kill, the generals directing them parasitically grow and build comfortable and happy lifestyles funded by fat-cat military budgets that the country can ill-afford.

They talk war, terrorism, "prevention of terrorism" to continue to get fat budgetary allocations for the military, while the common man in Pakistan and Kashmir struggles to get an education, a job and make ends meet.

The military spending only serves the motives of the generals. The economics of the army of Pakistan happily demands all these vulnerable elements pay with their sweat and blood for the extravagant lifestyles of the Pakistani Army Top Brass.

Such are the hidden agendas based on thinly veiled economics that drive war. If we really dig into the reasons for war since time immemorial, we would know that there are underlying and maybe hidden economic reasons to fight wars.

The fuse of the war machinery may be lit with numerous possible justifications to fool the public but the underlying cause has more often than not been wealth and power.

Asymmetric Warfare

*"If you use weapons of war to bring about peace,
you're going to have more war and destruction."*

- *Coretta Scott King*

*"I asked a Burmese why women, after centuries of following their men,
now walk ahead.
He said there were many unexploded land mines since the war."*

- *Robert Mueller*

'Asymmetric warfare' is an asymmetric engagement in a war between parties who differ greatly in military power, strategy or tactics. It could be a war between a professional army and even insurgents or resistance movements or unlawful combatants.

Correspondingly, it can be a fight between countries with unequal strengths, where one nation with lesser strength will exercise the use of these strategies and tactics to avoid playing into the strengths of a stronger adversary.

Asymmetric warfare may even include space-based surveillance and intelligence systems to gather data on adversaries that can be used in case of a conflict. Anti-satellite weapons, laser, microwave, anti-radar weapons and infrared decoys are all part of the mix.

In terms of insurgencies, it may involve the use of terrain, guerrilla hit and run tactics to trouble and demoralize the enemy.

Since the 1950s a number of insurgents and resistance movements have seen some success in keeping much larger forces and powers pinned down in spite of having inferior numbers and lesser sophistication of weapons.

Those with lesser power resort to asymmetric warfare as a means to take on a bigger and more powerful opponent. Asymmetric warfare is thus an adaptation of a lesser power to take on a bigger opponent.

Using new and unconventional ways, smaller forces are able to blunt the conventional superiority of the more powerful adversary. This is something that is here to stay because of the asymmetries in the conventional forces of the players around the world.

Irregular Warfare

"I am tired and sick of war. Its glory is all moonshine.
It is only those who have neither fired a shot nor heard the shrieks and groans of the wounded, who cry aloud for blood, for vengeance, for desolation.
War is hell."

- William Tecumseh Sherman

"Weapons are an important factor in war, but not the decisive one; it is man and not materials that counts."

- Mao Zedong

Since the cost of conventional or nuclear warfare is prohibitive, it is expected that weaker countries with the intent to avoid extensive damage to their military would employ what we call 'irregular warfare' to undercut the power and influence of their enemies.

'Irregular warfare' involves a combination of sophisticated cyber offensives, covert actions and information warfare. It also means providing support to state and non-state proxies in an attempt to undermine the enemy. This has been used by countries like Russia, North Korea, and Iran to undermine the enemy.

Some of the methods of irregular warfare include covert campaigns to support influential figures and opposition parties, targeted assassinations, bribery and underhand dealings to box the enemy into a corner.

These methods have been employed by various powers of the world. Israel and even the United States of America have used cyber-warfare and viruses to infiltrate enemies, for example, in Iran to create huge setbacks for their nuclear ambitions.

Countries such as China have long been accused of infiltrating networks of corporations and defence establishments in the west to steal intellectual property, military secrets and designs in order to 'steal a march' in the areas of high-end technology.

Over the years, many military hardware designs bearing an eerie similarity to comparable equipment created and designed in the west have surfaced from Chinese research establishments.

The US has often failed to protect its intellectual property and military secrets from Chinese and Russian cyber agents.

Economic warfare by denial of land routes, monopolization of sea routes and even as the creation of industrial unrest in enemy lands is a part of a concerted effort to unseat the enemy from a position of advantage. Some countries like Pakistan have even pumped counterfeit currency into enemy nations to weaken the economy of enemy countries.

The methods used include clandestine efforts that use social media to glean information with false profiles and honey traps to lure and extract information regarding enemy personnel etc.

Russia has been accused of meddling in the United States and UK elections by using proxies and pumping in money to buy influence on social media. Russia has also been accused of using honey traps and money to meddle in the affairs of enemy countries.

Terrorist outfits have also used social media tools such as Facebook to target and recruit gullible nationals around the world for their devious plans.

Videos on *Youtube* have been used to romanticize killing of non-believers and the propaganda videos have created an aura around terrorism with an attempt to attract and brainwash youth into joining these outfits.

Twitter has been used to reach out and stay on 'top of the mind' of potential recruits, causing them to be swayed by the 'calls of duty' to unleash terror. Messaging platforms have been widely used to organize and coordinate attacks on intended targets.

These methods of irregular warfare are low-cost measures that terrorists and even countries have taken to weaken and undercut the enemy. These methods offer the perpetrator deniability and limited liability.

Moreover, the country at the receiving end of the offensives is thrown off balance and would find it difficult to prevent or contain the ensuing damage to it. For these reasons such covert means of warfare have come into favour as preferred means to torment the enemy.

The high cost of direct conventional or nuclear warfare not only drives the adoption of these irregular methods but also, we are likely to see more and more of such tactics in the future.

New defensive measures to recognize and prevent such overt and covert irregular warfare would have to be devised to neutralize these methods in the future. What would happen is only to be seen.

Peace

"There is nothing that war has ever achieved
that
we could not better achieve without it."

- Havelock Ellis

"I cannot believe that war is the best solution.
No one won the last war,
and
no one will win the next war."

- Eleanor Roosevelt

"Be convinced that
to be happy means to be free and that
to be free means to be brave.
Therefore, do not take lightly the perils of war."

- Thucydides

The horrors of war are something that is familiar to those who have fought it and to those who were victims of collateral damage. Wars never really end. They are only paused. There is a constant struggle to gain the upper hand and devise more and more lethal weapons.

However, as the Mahatma (played by Ben Kinsley in the 1982 production directed by Richard Attenborough) had said, "An eye for an eye will only make the world go blind". There cannot be peace without trust and there cannot be trust without good intentions and humanity.

The warmongers may romanticize war but it is always to be remembered that war involves the spilling of the blood of thousands of innocents and it has no end.

However, given the distrust between nations, it only can be said that the greatest challenge and the most difficult fight is the battle against the evils of war. War would always try to rear its ugly head.

As nations continue to disbelieve other nations, the only way to prevent a war is to prepare for it. As the former missile scientist and former president of India, **Late A.P.J Abdul Kalam** had said,

"Only strength respects strength"

Only strength will deter an adversary. Sadly, this is the truth. Nations with even defensive intentions and pacifist principles will need to prepare for war more thoroughly to keep the upper hand and to maintain peace.

To prevent war, one needs to prepare for war itself. This along with noble intentions can be the only guarantor for peace.

"The Best way
to
Prevent a War,
Is to be
Prepared for One."

- Author

Conclusion

"War will never cease until babies begin to come into the world with larger cerebrums and smaller adrenal glands."

- H. L. Mencken

"War may sometimes be a necessary evil. But no matter how necessary, it is always an evil, never a good. We will not learn how to live together in peace by killing each other's children."

- Jimmy Carter

World War II was not the last war fought. However, since then, the world has been less violent because of the deterrence of the increasing sophistication of weapons and the notion of mutually assured destruction.

When compared to other periods of human history since the 1950s the costs of war and the potential damage it can do to economies have increased greatly and this has kept large scale wars limited.

Having said that, however, it is not that wars have been eliminated or that war will not happen. It is just that it will take a different shape in the form of asymmetric warfare and irregular warfare, where deniability and ability to limit culpability would embolden enemy states to spar at each other without direct confrontation.

More than a blitzkrieg we are going to see the slow bleeding and erosion of authority being employed by enemy states to counter stronger opponents. This is the new reality we have begun to recognize.

Since 9/11, the battlefield has shifted to new fronts, fought by enemies who shoot and scoot with no real global address or single commanding authority. Every time a central enemy figure has been eliminated a new one has emerged.

Challenges and the landscape have been constantly changing. To uproot completely and decisively this hydra headed monster, the world would require the coordinated effort of a number of like-minded nations.

PART III

Self-Improvement

Chapter 1

THE ESSENTIALS

Know the most basic building blocks of happiness

"Three grand essentials to happiness in this life are
something to do,
something to love,
and
something to hope for."

-Joseph Addison
(English writer 1672-1719)

"The First Essentials is of course to know what you want."

-Robert Colliner
(American Author 1885 - 1950)

It was the first day of the fall semester final exams. The year was 2004, and I was in the U.S., pursuing my M.B.A. course. The first exam was for a one credit course. It was meant to be a general introduction to the M.B.A. program. It was a three-hour exam and the students were informed of the exam question in advance.

The question was an open-ended one and was repeated year after year, but with slight twists. We all came well prepared for the question, lest there be a slight twist in the question this year. We were allowed to carry anything into the exam hall and I was all set.

As I entered the corridor, the professor of the course smiled at me and said "You're looking relaxed and ready". I answered in the affirmative and pointed at the large bag that I was wheeling into the exam hall. I said that I was confident and well equipped, no matter what twist would be thrown at me.

I took my seat and the exam began. The question was written on the board and was simple. It read, "What are the essentials you need to complete your course successfully? Justify". I knew by justification it meant that I was to attach proof. The professor then told us that this was an open-ended question and that there was no real correct answer.

So, I gathered the entire stack of papers and photos of the 'essentials' that I had previously taken a snap of and laid them out on the table. There was a huge pile on the table and in front of me. I had previously done my M.S. in engineering in the U.S. and had been quite clear about what I needed when I landed in the University to do my full time M.B.A.

I called it the '5 Cs' essentials. In fact, I maintained a folder called the '5 Cs'. It had subfolders which were the '5 Cs'. The Car, Computer (laptop), Cell (mobile phone), Camera (we did not have smart phones then) and Credit Card. Within the '5Cs' subfolders, I had maintained excel worksheets and other statements relating to fuel expenses, phone bills, credit card statements and photos.

So, I began my exam with the list that I had named as the '5 essentials'. These were the key 'essentials' I had zeroed in on even before I had landed in the US. Then, I set out to add other things to the list and went on to attach photos wherever I could. I thought, "Hey the winter coat was very important", "I definitely required heating", "How about books, writing pads, stationery including pens, stapler, stapler pins, glue?", "How about a stereo system to hear some music in my room?", "How about an ice maker, because I loved ice in my lemon tea come summer or winter?" and so on. I began to lose direction before I began to pull back.

Then, I thought "health" is most important. My mind began to ramble further and I thought water is essential. To avoid unhealthy pop, I needed to carry my own water. Hence, I needed a sturdy metal water bottle to lug around. I thought my answer was getting smarter. For maintaining my health, the fundamental tripod; *Sleep, Exercise* and *Healthy Food* was essential.

So, I thought I needed a comfortable mattress and pillow to keep good sleep hygiene. I would need to eat an apple everyday (to keep the doctor away). I would have to measure the calories burnt in the gym and so an electronic strap-on device (equipment of those days) to watch the calories I burnt was necessary. Additionally, I would need my gym gloves (for weights), towel, gym water bottle, cross training shoes, work-out pants and t-shirts and the list went on.

While I surmised good health was essential, I wondered about the other intangibles. As I deliberated on these my answers were tending to get more open ended. How about 'motivation', 'passion for the subjects', 'discipline' as essentials? I kept feeling like I was getting smarter and smarter with my answers and I began to think harder.

Suddenly, my stack of notes and photos were missing, they weren't in front of me or anywhere on my desk. I got up and went in search of them. I was told they were in the room down the hall and had been transferred there, as they were occupying too much space. I searched for a while until I found the room. They were stacked in the room alongside material brought in by the other candidates. By the time I sorted them out and returned to the exam hall, my time was up, I wasn't able to complete my exam.

I refused to hand in the exam paper and told the proctor that I had not written the answers to my satisfaction and would rather take the exam again next semester. This was an important question and I wanted to answer it after a lot of thought. The proctor said that unless, I finished this one credit course, I could not proceed with my other course work. I was having a debate and there was a heated exchange of words. Suddenly, the question on the class room board got reframed as "What are the essentials of life?" I was so shocked that I finally woke-up.

Being Awake and Alive

It was 2 a.m. and I had awakened from a strange dream, that also awakened something else within. This was a dream that had its roots in memories from about a decade ago. The actual one credit course I took in the 1st semester of my M.B.A. program was on 'Strategy'. In my dream, I had somehow reframed the question and had reframed the scenario. So, I sat up and began to re-analyse my dream and reframed the question; **"What is most important to me in LIFE?"**

The flowing melange of the logical and illogical in my dream world made for a strange combination of answers. However, while I lay awake and consciously pondered on this question, my answers were almost predictable. I moved to the computer and began to key in my thoughts. Understandably, my list began with family, my wife, my kids, my parents and then my siblings, and other family and friends.

Then at once I moved on to health, as 'Health is wealth'. The same health list involving essentials for good sleep and exercise formed part of my list. My sub-conscious self that wrote dreamy notes were in sync, I couldn't stress more on the importance of **sleep**, **exercise** and **healthy food**; the **fundamental tripod**. This tripod forms the foundation for a good life and stands ahead of every other essential.

If family and friends are like one's flesh and blood, one's good health would form the very bones in this body of life. To be able to function independently without being a burden or an outcast, one needs the wealth of good health. In fact, these would form the backbone of life ahead of anything else. Family and friends are the flesh and blood without which there is no life to the body. However, we still do need the bone structure to stand up and function without being a burden to others. Family and good health are **two of the three** most essentials for a good life.

What could then be the **third** essential? What else did one need? As I pondered, I keyed in a list that came to my mind. In most cases people would like to have:

i. Work life balance

ii. More leisure time

iii. Time with family

iv. Time to pursue one's passions

v. Job satisfaction or should I reframe it as 'Life Satisfaction'

vi. Ability to live in the moment without worrying about the past or future

A closer examination of the list revealed a single thread that may be common for all. To have more 'free' time or to be engaged in work that one enjoyed, rather than to be consumed by work that is thrust on them, there was one other need. People would definitely like more free time and would like to be engaged in work that they chose, rather than being obliged to work. This is where I would like to introduce the concept of finance. This sense of stress-free time in the pursuit of happiness and life satisfaction is achieved by a certain something that would maintain the stability of an individual's life. From the prism of finance, it has a name. It is called 'FINANCIAL FREEDOM'.

'Financial freedom' would help one achieve this list. Money does make this list possible. If one had financial freedom, one could have more free time and leisure. One could choose a job with more work life balance. One could pursue one's passions and one could take care of one's family and health. Moreover, when we do follow our passion, "work" would no more be like work and it would be transformed into something fun. It wouldn't become a daily drudgery but instead become something one looked forward to.

If one had 'FINANCIAL FREEDOM', a lot of what I had said above, would fall in place automatically. **'Financial freedom' is when one has the bandwidth to stop worrying about money and start living life to one's fullest potential and desires**. It is not necessarily a huge quantum of money but it is the point where **money stops being a factor**, and it **is different for different people**. However, one could calibrate that point by understanding and adjusting one's needs, desires and focusing on what one would really need to do to achieve the goal of being happy.

So, to begin with, the THREE ESSENTIALS of a happy life are:

i. 'HEALTH'

ii. 'FRIENDS & FAMILY' and

iii. 'FINANCIAL FREEDOM'.

Chapter 2

HOW MUCH DO YOU NEED TO BE HAPPY?

Why the definition of happiness is in your own hands and how best to define it

---

"The real measure of your wealth is
how much you'd be worth
if you lost
all your money."

- *Anonymous*

"It is not the man who has too little,
but the man who craves more,
that is poor."

- *Lucius Annaeus Seneca*

There was once a billionaire who was staying in a penthouse with his wife and young child. His home was lavish with an indoor pool, indoor personal home theatre and all other trappings of a billionaire's lifestyle.

The home was a spacious penthouse with a massive flowing hall, eight large bedrooms, a private bar, a private study and private elevator to get atop the skyscraper.

The billionaire's son was spoilt as he was accustomed to all the luxuries. The young boy often threw tantrums much to the vexation of the billionaire father. The son was always stuck to the mobile phone, television or computer, playing games and whiling away precious time by mindlessly watching videos.

The rich father wanted the child to know the value of things and hence decided to take the child on a three-day trip to his simple native village where the inhabitants lived frugally.

He wanted the child to see his simple beginnings, appreciate how far he had come and how happy and grateful they need to be, to have such a rich lifestyle. He desired that his child would realize and see the hardships that he had borne before he became who he is now. He wanted his son to see the trials and tribulations of life, the struggles and consequent challenges, the sorrows and difficulties that a common person goes through in his/her life.

Hence one day, they drove hundreds of miles out of the city, deeper and deeper into the countryside. Once they had reached their village, the billionaire and his son got off their vehicle and decided to camp on the outskirts of the village. They spent three gruelling days in which the son spent his time meeting the villagers and living their life.

He would walk with them and help draw water out of the well. He spent time in the fields helping with the harvest of crops and vegetables. He learnt how to milk the cows. He immersed himself in the chores and games of the village kids. After sundown, like birds, the children would return to their nests. As they sat down on the floor for their early dinner, they would hear village elders' fascinating stories mixed with rustic songs. They then retired outside on their rope cot beds or simple mats spread in the courtyard. The billionaire father watched all of this with satisfaction.

On the fourth day, they packed up their belongings and began their drive back home. As they drove back, the billionaire asked his son how his experience was and what he thought of the difficult and poor lives of the villagers. The son looked perplexed and responded by saying that the villagers lived luxurious lives. This mystified the billionaire. "How is that?" he asked amused.

The son began to list a few things. He said he would miss sleeping under the open sky, watching out for shooting stars and breathing in the gentle grass touched breeze. He said his air-conditioning in the pent house wasn't as 'cool'.

He said the milk was fresh and he enjoyed the fresh vegetables that he plucked. He loved its taste more than what he ate in the city or at fancy restaurants. His father then thought that the food was indeed fresh and the fruits and vegetables were organic. On the other hand, he thought we ate processed foods and drank soft drinks from cans, plastic packaging and pet bottles.

He also thought that as city dwellers, they drank water and carbonated drinks from pet bottles, while the villagers found use for every small thing, recycling or down-cycling even simple clothes that would be used until they were rags for cleaning or wiping. This took care of the environment too, unlike the waste and trash that cities generated and found difficult to dispose.

His thoughts were interrupted as the child spoke animatedly about bathing in the streams and swimming in the lake. He said it was not at all like the private indoor swimming pool they had. The indoor pool had water that was stagnant and smelt of chemicals while the lake was expansive and the streams were crystal clear and flowing. His father understood that the child was referring to the chlorine in the pools when he said chemicals.

The villagers lived amongst the green and with nature in a serene atmosphere surrounded by mountains, streams and fresh air. In contrast, they lived in a polluted city, pigeonholed into their pent-house.

The villagers spent time playing board games and the children had simple toys made of readily available materials which allowed them to use their imagination. They spent a lot of time outdoors in the sun and the open without their fancy play stations and multiple gadgets.

The child then mentioned the stories he had heard and asked why he didn't get as much time with adults and neighbours? He liked that all the villagers lived as a community and spent time together every evening. He loved the stories, music and chalk drawn games played with little stones.

As the child spoke his father thought how this was again in stark contrast to their own lives where one only interacted on social media and did not even know one's neighbour. The child's delight expressed a yearning for time together, with family as a community; something that we miss in our hurried lives spent chasing the next million dollars.

The billionaire was completely taken aback by his son's answers. He had brought him to teach him something about the 'real' world. The child in his unbiased manner had made unconditioned factual observations that astounded him and taught him something in turn. The billionaire had to admit that it is NOT money alone that makes one wealthy. He learnt a lot from the experiences of his child.

This story only illustrates the many different dimensions to wealth and happiness. While we are conditioned and bombarded with images of success, happiness and methods of celebration advertised and projected by both media and society, we forget to experience or think of some of the simple pleasures in our lives.

We are conditioned by the media and society to believe that we cannot be happy without all the trappings of modern living and that we cannot be happy until we achieve the billionaire status and we own that private jet. This is far from the truth.

One actually defines one's happiness. The story is to make one realise that **we could decide how much we want and what could make us actually happy**. Happiness lies within **our definition of our needs** and this could be anything or nothing. Then, when we do define these needs, the question that would then arise is; "What do we need to give up in pursuit of these needs?"

The intention is neither to sound philosophical nor to say that one needs to live like a villager. That is unnecessary, impractical, and also impossible for all of us. The story only seeks to differentiate between the:

- NEEDS,
- WANTS
- LUXURIES.

We need to first make a list of what we would consider as our 'NEEDS', what we would define as our 'WANTS' and what would fall under the category of 'LUXURIES'.

This would then help us categorize, reduce and eliminate those that fall under luxuries, maybe cancel a few wants only to lead happier lives in pursuit firstly of our needs. This would also make us take cognisance of what we would be 'giving up' in exchange for each of our 'needs' 'wants' and 'luxuries'. To illustrate let's look at examples of some 'needs' and see if they are actual 'needs.'

For instance, do we ask if five bedrooms are truly necessary? Could we do well with a two- or three-bedroom home? Do we all really care about changing cars every three years? Do we really need that luxury car and private pool? Do we need to put in overtime and trade it for our leisure and time with family?

Do we actually need those 'things' we buy with all the extra-earnings from over-time? Even if we could afford all these trappings, do these really add to our happiness? These are pertinent questions to ask. More money does not necessarily equate to more happiness.

Now everyone is different and will have a different answer. Some may live within $30,000/year some need $10,000,000/year. Are we trading our happiness for more money? Are we trading our leisure?

Are we trading our time with family and friends? Are we too pre-occupied to set aside time for our health and fitness?

While we do compromise and make sacrifices, are we forced to let go of our old hobbies, interests and other pursuits? Are we slowly forgetting our passions and life goals?

If the answers to these questions are "yes" then do we need to cut down on our luxuries to lead happier and holistic lives? We need to answer these questions and answer them honestly to ascertain where our happiness equation and equilibrium stand.

It is necessary for us to understand that there are 'MANY KINDs of Wealth'.

- MONEY,
- STATUS,
- TIME,
- FAMILY,
- FRIENDS AND HEALTH

Are individual pillars in their own right.

The question is "Are we sacrificing the last four (TIME, FAMILY, FRIENDS & HEALTH) while we seek to achieve the first two (MONEY & STATUS)?" and can we find a balance to maximise our happiness?

We need to know our happiness formula, where we add and/or subtract 'needs', 'wants' and 'luxuries', to multiply our sense of contentment and happiness. The definition of wealth is limited when we choose to use only money and status as the measure.

Pleasure, satisfaction, contentment and happiness are all nuanced emotions that we are driven to achieve through a multi-pronged approach.

The nuances of money and status have many projected trappings, faces, notions that are sometimes make-believe and pretty. They are "states" that one hopes to achieve and are beautifully crafted to seem just out of reach, such that one ends up constantly chasing them like a mirage.

We see it daily on different screens promoted by our media, society and peer group. They slowly seep into our mind and eat away our imagination. We need to unlearn these, and de-condition ourselves, only to ascertain what OUR own formula is, so that we could make our own path, in pursuit of "happiness".

It is not necessary to expand one's possessions at the expense of the other pillars of our lives to achieve happiness. Happiness sometimes lies in balancing ambition with contentment.

As **Epictetus** once stated,

"As wealth consists not in having great possessions,
but in having
few wants".

Chapter 3

QUANTUM OF HAPPINESS

Know the real secret to happiness in the modern world and how a change in outlook could make you happy

---

"The happiest people in the world are NOT those who have the best of things, but those who know how to appreciate the things they have the best."

- *Warren Buffett*

"Happiness is a choice, not a result.
Nothing will make you happy until you choose to be happy,
No person will make you happy unless you decide to be happy.
Your happiness will not come to you. It can only come from you."

- *Ralph Harslon*

I was working in a management position for a company in one of my stints. I happened to have had a very capable junior colleague working for me. He was a top performer, who was young and was on a handsome salary for his age group.

He was treated very well. Yet, one day he came into my cabin and began to pour out his frustrations to me.

He said that he was very unhappy with his life and felt very dissatisfied despite having all the material goodies. I asked him if his salary was the reason. He replied in the negative and said that he did not have a clear understanding of why he was unhappy.

He had been given a raise of more than 30% year on year for the past three years. He had all the material trappings a young man in his twenties would desire. He had a nice car, latest mobile phones, home theatre system, nice apartment which was well furnished etc., I enquired about his lifestyle.

He ate out, hung out with friends, went to movies and played many console games like any other young person of his age. Yet, he felt incomplete and amiss. He said nothing seemed to interest him and he felt low.

David Foster Wallace put this outlook in perspective when he said, **"In this country (U.S.A) we're unprecedentedly safe, comfortable, and well fed, with more and better venues for stimulation. And yet if you were asked, 'Is this a happy or unhappy country?' you'd check the 'unhappy' box. We're living in an era of emotional poverty, which is something that serious drug addicts feel most keenly"**.

We belong to a generation that could achieve instant gratification on an impulse. We are part of that age and it is easy to feel dissatisfied, and nothing seems to make us feel sufficiently satiated. Our highs and excitement are short lived, it was consumed yesterday and we look forward to the next one immediately. It isn't easy to appreciate what we have and we often get bored too soon.

I felt I needed to step back to analyse and re-evaluate his state of things. I then went on to tell **him about how good his life actually was.** He needed to, and well, we all needed to understand **why we should appreciate our lives better.**

In this modern era, our lives and lifestyles are actually better than the lifestyles of the rich and powerful kings who reigned our lands just a few of hundred years ago. Kings and emperors who built lavish castles and reigned supreme over several kingdoms wouldn't have had the comfort that we have today.

Today, our lifestyle is rich, comfortable, and adventurous without risk and is filled with the choicest of options and variety that no king could have commanded. This young colleague was both intrigued and sceptical, yet he asked me to explain more. I began to explain each scenario.

When the kings of yore wanted to listen to music what were the ways they could get what they wanted? Musicians would need to be arranged and at the appointed time they would arrive and play music. On the other hand, nowadays, one could listen to music and any kind of music at the touch of a screen.

Music from around the world, all genres from pop, classical, hip-hop, blues, jazz, melody and so on are all at one's disposal. We could go encore, stop, start, skip, switch in a jiffy. We could also choose to hear it on headphones or stereos if we wished, at the prescribed volume and even adjust the acoustics with greater bass or more treble, without even moving from our chair. Even today's live performances and 'shows' offer limitless entertainment with visual effects, laser lights shows, while the experience of yesteryear kings would seem "poor" with their highly limited options.

Similarly, name any other kind of entertainment, dance, theatre, or the court jester of old times, they have all been replaced and are now made available in better larger than life formats. It was previously limited to the king and his courts. We live lives filled with entertainment that could be obtained, consumed and enjoyed so easily by all, at a flick of a switch.

If we were to travel like the way the kings travelled before, it would probably take a lot of motivation and possibly a lot of strength and stamina. The kings travelled miles across plains and mountains on horseback, chariot drawn vehicles or caravans which were extremely bumpy rides.

Travelling kings were exposed to the elements, bore heat and cold on horsebacks leaving them with sore behinds. They would either get sun baked or be cold and stiff depending on the weather.

Today, travel is a leisure activity, not a tough work out (unless we choose to go hiking or cycling). In the modern era, it is pleasurable to travel for work or holiday. We could sit on a comfortable car seat and drive smoothly in an air-conditioned car equipped with shock absorbers that plied on smooth bitumen layered roads.

To add to our royal travel, we would be able listen to the finest choice of music from our personal collection or simply turn on the radio while we travel. In this manner, we could easily cover great distances in style with little fatigue. The king's travel experience actually pales in comparison to this.

Having an appetite and being king still had limitations. Pre-arranged menus, the search for ingredients and the seasonal availability of fruits, vegetables and spices would remain as constraints. We have food ordering applications and food guides which could cater to us on the spur of the moment.

They would provide us with food from the choicest of restaurants. Cuisines and variety that were unheard of are available for us, allowing us to be as finicky as a royal. We could choose Chinese, Italian, Mexican, Indian, Thai and other cuisines from around the world. We could cherry-pick and either have fast food, gourmet fare or a healthy mix anytime of the day.

Legend has it that Philippides or Pheidippides, the Greek messenger was sent to Athens to announce the defeat of the Persians. Athens was about 42.195 Kms. away from his destination. He ran the whole distance to say his famous last words "Niki! Niki!" (Victory! Victory!), before he collapsed to his death, thus sharing the news of the Grecian victory in the Battle of Marathon. That's how kings got their news. Expensive and sometimes life threatening.

For information and entertainment in the modern era, we get alerts delivered directly onto our handsets, or we could seek them out easily off the web. We have several options and several screens, televisions, tablets, and e-readers. We could order online and read e-versions, or order them to be delivered at our doorsteps. The king on the other hand, would depend on foot soldiers, horseback messengers, or ships, boatmen and spies to deliver information that may have taken days to pass on.

Singapore's founding father Mr. Lee Kuan Yew thought that the single biggest secret reason for Singapore's success was the invention of air-conditioning. It changed the nature of civilization by making development possible in the tropics. Apart from comfort and increased efficiency at work, air conditioning allowed for people to migrate and live in inhospitable climates.

Inventions like refrigeration allowed one to eat the choicest fruits and vegetables brought from far off lands. Also, we could easily store food in refrigerators and cabinets to be eaten as desired. Even simple pleasures like a glass of cold water or a cup of ice-cream would have been a luxury for the kings of those days.

Even not so far back as a hundred years ago, the only way the royals could enjoy an iced drink in the tropics was by constructing an 'ice-house' and transporting ice from afar to be stored and retrieved from this ice house. Those days and times were truly difficult and it was truly challenging to enjoy these simple pleasures which we now take for granted.

Entertainment would either be adrenaline driven wars or hunting campaigns.

Of course the Romans used gladiators to fight each other and we have truly come a long way from those barbaric times.

Nowadays, if one needed to be entertained, one could go to amusement parks, catch a movie in a theatre, organize game nights with play stations and so on. War games, virtual reality, augmented reality games amuse and entertain us and cause little harm to our fellow beings, while we get the same rush without having to nurse deep wounds in the aftermath.

Kings and Queens would send explorers and scientists to research and view the world through their eyes. Long distance travel by both ship and horseback was tough. One was exposed to difficult conditions, elements of nature and attacks by wild animals. Nowadays, we could jet around the world in a fraction of the time, and choose to stay in different types of accommodations such as hotels, lodges, home stays etc.

We wear the choicest of clothing and footwear. Not to mention the wide range of accessories that are available in malls and bazaars. We could even shop on our couch while we browse online and order merchandise to be home delivered.

In every facet technologies have increased our comfort and conveniences by many folds in our lives. When we compare the kind of medical care and preventive medicine available for us today with what was available for the kings and queens of yester years, we are far more privileged and blessed.

We could also learn arts, music, dance, martial art forms, do aerobics, learn yoga at our convenience or even online. All these are made possible in convenient and affordable ways.

If we were to just get down to the basics even a good bath under a decent shower and flush toilets were a luxury in those days.

Whether it is learning music, gathering knowledge, access to books, information, travel, food, health care, entertainment, WE ARE TRULY LIVING LIKE KINGS AND QUEENS!!!

These words and scenarios made my junior colleague's eye light-up, I could see he was re-evaluating his life. The possessions and advantages didn't change and were always there but the change that was necessary was **in his attitude and approach, which was what he required.**

Over the next few days I could see that change in the way he was, he didn't get despondent. To be happy, we really need to first be happy with what we have before we crave for more. As Warren Buffett once famously said, "**The happiest people in the world are NOT those who have the best of things, but those who know how to appreciate the things they have the best**".

We have come a long way from what our forefathers were and the kind of lifestyles they led. I don't denigrate the lives of kings and queens, but only bring about those scenarios to show how royally advantaged we are. We benefit from the work and progress made by several generations. They have made us what we are today, yet when we don't understand or appreciate how far we have come, where we were and where we now are, it would be difficult for us to further the progress.

A number of cultures teach us to respect and appreciate what we are given. Almost every culture teaches us to say a prayer of thanks before we eat. This is widely prevalent in many religions. Festivals giving thanks are celebrated world over, as either harvest festivals, thanks giving or festivals that offer gratitude. They all help us realise and appreciate every bounty in our lives from agricultural produce, our families, animals, books, tools of work etc.

A variety of cultures practice these to ingrain a sense of gratitude so we realise how lucky we are for receiving such bounties. It is not necessarily just to praise GOD, but as an introspection to make us look within and to find happiness, as those who are thankful, understand the true value of what they actually have, before they begin to seek more and more. Such people are the happiest.

We need to incorporate these notions into our lives, where we introspect to first respect and cherish what we have, before getting despondent about what we don't have. Therein rests the secret to happiness. We need to find that sense of contentment first and then happiness would follow automatically. This certainly doesn't mean we hold down our ambitions. **We just shouldn't let ambition and greed come in the way of our happiness today.**

While finance is an essential component of happiness, it does not guarantee happiness. Our attitude will determine how happy we are or how happy we will be. This is why blind materialism does not lead to happiness, because materialism is an endless chasm and we would sacrifice our happiness today in pursuit of something that we think will make us happy and complete tomorrow. That never happens because it is in our nature to desire and greed for more.

As a wise man once said,

"Now and then it is better to pause in our pursuit of happiness
and
just be happy."

Happiness is a function of your approach and attitude and finance has a limited role to play in it. So, while finance is important, our approach to life is most important.

Having the 'right attitude' and having 'gratitude'
are the
TWO keys to happiness.

Chapter 4

LIVING WITHIN YOUR MEANS

How to categorise and define your spending to put yourself on the road to 'Financial Freedom'

"If you buy things that you do not need,
soon you will have to sell things you need."

- Warren Buffett

"How rich you are is NOT defined by
HOW MUCH you spend,
but by
HOW MUCH you save."

- Author

Middle class parents around the world have **advised their children** on the **dangers of overspending** and **living beyond their means**. While this **is sound advice**, one really needs to **dissect and define** what this **means.** One also needs to **present it in a fashion** that the **young spenders** would **understand and adopt. Children** of such parents often **hit back or rebel** when advised about their spending. They see it as an **infringement on** their **right to happiness** that the material things could bring.

Hence, there is a need to **help children define and understand** that some money is to be spent for **immediate needs and happiness**, while some needs to be **saved and invested** for the future. It's **a balance. Delayed gratification** can sometimes have benefits as the **invested money** can **grow manifold** and **provide stability** and **hence happiness.**

Before one were to venture out to invest, one first **needs to save.** One also needs to save to **gradually build a 'Reserve'**, which would **serve as a cushion** in bad times. It would also **help to build a 'Nest Egg'** that would ensure that there is a **perpetual inflow of money** in the form of **'Passive income'**. When this 'Passive income' is **sufficiently high** it would **lead to financial liberation** and what I call **'Financial Freedom'**. To be **able to save** however, one **needs to understand** how one **spends his/her money**. Spending **has to be dissected** to **understand** as to whether its **contribution to happiness** is **commensurate.**

Handling your Expense Account

"We lost our way and allowed greed and excess to become the twin pillars of too much of the financial culture. We became a society utterly absorbed in consumption and dismissive of moderation."

- Tom Brokaw

"I'd like to live as a poor man with lots of money."

- Pablo Picasso

The **first advice** to any one **handling or budgeting** for an **expense account** is to **divide one's expenses** into one of the **three categories:**

- Needs
- Wants
- Luxuries

The names are pretty descriptive. **'Needs'** are essentially those items in our expense account which are **needed for basic living.** One needs to pay rent or our mortgage. One needs to pay the utility and fuel bills. One needs food, clothing etc.

'Wants' are those **things that one desires** that **could make one happier** but are those things that one **probably could do without**. So basically, one may want to change car every three years, but one really doesn't NEED to. One may want to drive a bigger SUV but one really doesn't need it. If one does make the purchase, then one would probably end up paying higher insurance and have higher fuel bills.

One may want a bigger five-bedroom house, but one may actually be single and one could do with a two-bedroom house that one could share with a room-mate. Actually, one's 'need' is accomplished by a two-bedroom house but one desires or 'wants' a five-bedroom house. Now, with a five-bedroom house one could end up paying higher property taxes, higher utility bills and one **may have to work harder** to maintain the home etc.

One's **'needs'** are **what one NEEDs**, while one's **'wants'** are **what one DESIREs.** Desires are something that would be **nice to have**. Not **all 'wants' are necessary,** and **could be eliminated** depending on whether it **makes sense,** and if it **really contributes** to **one's happiness**. Often, **'wants' should be treated** as **items of delayed gratification** and should only be **procured or attained** after a long wait. It should be treated as **reward for one's hard work**. The **wait** would **increase** our **desire and happiness** when one ultimately acquires or experiences one's reward.

'Luxuries' are those that one **shouldn't try to acquire** if it **stretches one's budget** or if one **has to sacrifice something** else like leisure or one has **to work much harder** to obtain. For example, one may commit to buying a luxury vehicle but may end up having to work harder for the next 5-7 years trying to pay off a depreciating asset. Another example is first class travel or international holidays.

Generally, **unless my passive income** is **paying off** such luxuries, these are just that **'luxuries'**. If one had to **draw from one's active income** (income from working) to pay for them, then one would **rather forego them**. It makes **very little sense** to pay for these **via active income** or pay for the same by **committing a heavy monthly EMI**.

Another example is expensive jewellery. **Weddings** and engagements are truly once in a lifetime celebration (at least that's our belief and hope). However, if that big ticket themed wedding with the large diamond engagement ring is **truly out of one's spending capacity**, one **should not fall into debt** just for it. This is particularly true if it **is going to chain us to our work** and cut down on any **possibility to save** for the future. Rather than extravagant spending, one could let **weddings** also be **occasions** where one **sows the seeds** for **financial growth**. Love should grow with the people one is in love with. Impressing the fiancée by buying that BIG diamond may be great. However, one needs to ask ourselves if it **is a need, want or luxury** in an objective manner.

There is an interesting study that says that the bigger the engagement ring and more the money spent on the wedding; on an average, the shorter the marriage. It is **not some paradox**, but is **actually logical**. Marriages that **start out with larger debts** are often **financially strained** and hence, are more likely to end badly.

A 'Sanskrit Slokha' that

conveys the power of simple living

सुखं शेते सत्यवक्ता सुखं शेते मितव्ययी ।

हितभुक् मितभुक् चैव तथैव विजितेन्द्रिय: ॥ - चरकसंहिता

***sukhaṃ śētē satyavaktā sukhaṃ śētē mitavyayī* ।**

***hitabhuk mitabhuk caiva tathaiva vijitēndriya:* ॥**

Meaning:

One who speaks truth sleeps well, one who spends less sleeps well.

One who eats nutritious food in limited quantity and one who has control over the mind and senses also gets peaceful sleep.

The **objective** of this piece is **not to tell people** to **spend less**. That is hardly what this is all about. Everyone's **situation is unique** and each one of us operates from different financial backgrounds. It is important to be **aware of the divisions** between **needs, wants and luxuries** for us individually, from our own standpoints. The danger is an oft repeated 'question'.

We often choose to act only based on that constant question that stays on our minds; "What will others say?" It is better to **spend only when** we can **afford to.** It is not advisable to spend only to impress others. When in doubt we need to ask ourselves, if that **spending** would **truly contribute** to our **long-term happiness** and **well-being.**

The **media** and **our peer group** would often **make us feel incomplete.** There is **constant bombardment** by corporations and media. They seem to tell us **why we need** to do this and **how it could** make us feel happy and complete. I don't blame them, that's their job and they do it beautifully, but we must be aware that it is **just pure marketing.** They **want us to feel incomplete** so that **they could sell us more** and more things that **we actually don't need.** So **before one buys** a product or service one needs to **ask oneself** some **honest questions.**

- Do I **really need** to buy this, will I **really use** it?
- Will it really **make me happy** in the **long term** or is it an impulse?
- Am I **giving up more** than I **gain**?

Before signing a cheque for a $100 or more my dad often advised me to pause and calmly ponder if I really needed it. The idea was to **pay attention** to the **dollars and pounds** and **NOT** be **'penny wise and pound foolish'**.

We need to **pay more attention** to **big ticket** items like renting, buying a house or car, buying jewellery, electronics or appliances or paying for education etc. **Smaller items** that add up could be **weighed against what they give us** in return. We definitely should **not buy stuff on impulse** for the sake of it, especially those things which we barely use.

My **American officemate** went on a **sabbatical** to a **third world** country. She **came back happier** with a **better perspective of life.** Just after her return, she **sold half the things** that she had in her house. After her trip she had **come to the realisation** that she **did not need most of the things** that she thought she could not do without. They were just adding to the trash in her house.

As she **disposed them**, she felt **lighter and mentally happier.** Her experience is an example to highlight the fact that most people often **buy or acquire** things they **really do not need.** They then have to **work harder and**

longer to pay for their spending 'sins'. This **greatly delays or postpones** indefinitely their **arrival** to the milestone of **'Financial Freedom'** and **liberation.**

So, let me spell out a **few rules** that could help:

- **Divide spending** into 'needs', 'wants' and 'luxuries.'
- **Eliminate the 'luxuries'** unless it can be paid for by 'Passive income' (Income coming from return on investments for which we do not have to put in active work).
- **Prune the 'wants'** to things that **really give** one **'Value for the Money'** or 'Bang for the Buck'. **Avoid impulsive purchases** of wants to avoid randomly splurging on things we really don't need. Do **spend on a *few* wants** that **really make you happy**. It is **best when wants** are **delayed and treated as items of delayed gratification.** It should often be as a **reward for things well done.** The wait and final acquisition would be **truly rewarding** and would make one happier than the short-lived pleasure derived from an impulsive purchase.

When one does follow these rules, one could **balance** one's **happiness** with one's **savings**. Savings should be **invested to grow** the **'Passive income'** that could be earned from it. 'Passive income' would further **ease our financial position** and **take us closer** to **'Financial Freedom'**.

This is one good way to lay out a **practical and effective** financial plan.

Chapter 5

UNDERSTANDING THE 'POWER OF COMPOUNDING'

Compounding has the power to turbo charge your investments

"The power of compounding is so great that our first job as investors is to avoid anything that might short circuit it."

- *Ira Rothberg*

"Compounding is the eighth wonder of the world. He who understands it, Earns it. He who doesn't, Pays it."

- *Albert Einstein*

Once upon a time, there was a king of a very rich kingdom. One day, an intelligent young scholar approached the king and introduced him to a new game of strategy and intelligence. The Game was called '*Satranj*' or chess. The king was mighty pleased with the game and asked the young man how he should be rewarded. The young scholar said he would like a few coins of gold be given to him but in a certain fashion.

He asked for one coin of gold to be placed on the first square of the chess board and double of that number to be placed on the second square. The third square should have double the number of coins on the second square. Double of the number of gold coins placed on the third was to be placed on the fourth square and so on doubling the amounts along the way until the sixty fourth square.

The king was amused and readily agreed to pay the scholar the said coins of gold according to the formula. He instructed his treasurer to release to the young man his prize according to this arrangement.

Later, much to the king's dismay the treasurer reported that the entire treasury was insufficient for the king to keep his promise. The king was taken aback. If this surprised you too, consider this, the sixty fourth square alone would've had to have 9,223,372,036,854,780,000 coins of gold for the arrangement to be satisfied. That's the 'Power of Compounding'. In this case, compounding happens at 100%.

This story serves to highlight the significance of compounding and its very powerful role in wealth generation. Warren Buffett once said **"My wealth has come from a combination of living in America, some lucky genes, and *compound interest*"**. He is absolutely right. Warren Buffett had two secrets.

The **first** is, he allowed the magic of compounding to work to the fullest of extents by making long term bets and staying invested in those investments over long periods of time.

The **second** thing most people often miss out on was that by staying invested, he deferred taxation thus allowing the entire sum to work and compound for him. When one constantly shuffles his/her investment, capital gains tax would flow out and reduce the sum gained and hence hinder the compounding of one's wealth. These two simple principles allowed for the power of compounding to work its magic to the fullest extent.

Have you heard an older gentleman brag "You know I bought this plot for only Rs. 25,000 in the year 1975, but in 2015 it was worth Rs. 10 Crores (1 Crore = 10 million)?" This has made many young investors gape in awe; their mobile phones cost more than Rs. 25,000 and the previous generation of investors had converted that much cash into what would be the worth of about 20 BMWs today!!! That's something. If one actually works it out, it would be about 23% compounded return from the year 1975.

The trick that happened is actually three-fold. The first is of course the fact that the older gentleman stayed invested for that long and the second is that he did not encash his property at any time during the 40-year period or shuffle his portfolio. He did not sell and hence did not lose money by paying capital gains taxes. This allowed for the entire sum to compound, rather than a sum that was diminished due to outflows. This was sufficient to propel his investment further and further until it was significant. The third was really because of 'low base effect'. When he started out, the amount invested was rather small. Hence, in the end his compounded return of 23% seems impressive when compared to his initial investment.

One caveat to note is that on the flip side, inflation also compounds and erodes your investment at an equally fast clip. Therefore, it is necessary to stay ahead of it. The real secret to making money in real estate is to stay invested for long periods and be prepared for lengthy investment horizons to see substantial returns. It is also necessary to choose your investments carefully. It is to be noted that nowadays (2018) the prices are ahead of fundamentals and the high base effect (larger quantum of investments) is something to contend with.

Hence, if the prices are already high to start with, it would be difficult to attain the spectacular returns, which was achieved, by the older gentleman we had spoken of. However, one could maximise returns by staying invested over a longer term and by investing in high growth properties.

Unlike stock investments, one of the things about investing in real estate is that one does not check on one's investments on a daily basis. Years later, when one does check on them, they seem to have grown significantly. This is really because of compounding.

However, if it does happen that inflation has galloped while one's investments have crawled; as it happens during times of stagflation (stagnation in growth in the economy and high inflation), one needs to be ready to face the damaging effect and the wrath of compounding. It would water down one's investments in no time. That is why even stagnation in real estate prices could heavily erode one's investment.

So, the next time you invest, keep the 'Power of Compounding' in mind. It has the power to create and the power to destroy wealth over a period of time.

Chapter 6

INVEST IN EXPERIENCES AND PEOPLE AND NOT IN MATERIAL ACQUISITIONS

How experiences and investing in people trumps material acquisitions and how investing in them increases your happiness manifold

---

"Materialism is the only form of distraction from true bliss."

- *Douglas Horton*

"Acquisition means life to miserable mortals."

- *Hesiod*

For most people money is a limited resource and the question that crops up is how to best allocate it to maximize one's happiness. Should we spend it on 'Material acquisitions' or on 'Experiences'? Material possessions last longer, a holiday would last a week or at best ten days, hence most people tend to prefer material possessions. How long do holidays actually last? Could we say material acquisitions are better as they last longer?

When I was dating, one of the questions I would ask my date would be "Given a bounty of $100,000, how would you spend it? Would you rather buy a new BMW? Or would you prefer to go on seven holidays over a seven-year period?" The answer to this question gave me an insight into whether I would like to go out with that person.

If the person said she would rather spend time with me on a holiday than in a BMW, I would go on to think we have matching thought processes. Personally, I value a holiday more than a BMW in the garage.

A holiday with your loved one would leave you with memories and shared experiences which would be talking points for decades to come. It could have wonderful or adventurous memories, shared escapades and all these create bonds that would last you a lifetime. Reliving those wonderful moments and talking about them would also create points of conversation and special bonds which would make us happier and more complete.

Decades later, it's more likely that holiday experiences with photos, videos of the experience could be relived with animated discussions on the experience. Decades later the memory of a BMW or any other luxury car in the garage would be less exciting. I rest my case.

I believe spending money on experiences contributes to happiness far more than spending on material things. I knew a couple in their 40s who were bickering and on the verge of splitting up. Nevertheless, they decided to go on a holiday together. Two weeks later they came back arm in arm unable to get enough of each other. Their closeness and bonding grew with their shared experience. A holiday is something a *Mastercard* could buy, but the bonding is certainly priceless.

While I may prefer and independently advice people to spend more on experiences and holidays, I have also found that research has also pointed in the same direction. Most people who are given a choice, choose material acquisitions such as jewellery or expensive cars over experiences. This is because most people believe material acquisitions just last longer than a one-off experience. This is a very logical conclusion indeed, yet the assumption on which the conclusion is based is actually flawed. Research suggests that the spending on trips, concerts or activities, dine-outs provide us with greater joy and satisfaction which would last longer.

One of the elements of human nature to consider is our ability to get accustomed and to adapt. While we buy new things to make us happy, they make us happy only for a while. They are exciting at first but then, we adapt to them and get used to them quickly. This diminishes the happiness that our new acquisitions gave us in the first place. Therefore, most psychologists suggest that it is better to spend our money on experiences.

We could go outdoors, visit a beach, go trekking, try hand gliding, do bungee jumping, go fine dining, travel, learn a new language or skill, visit art exhibits. We have endless options. Indulging in the next big impulsive purchase like buying the next generation phone or a luxury sports car would not however lead to lasting happiness.

Research has also found that when we make either a material purchase or buy an experience, the initial excitement is the same. Over time however, people's satisfaction with material things fade and fizzle out. On the contrary people's satisfaction with experiences goes up.

Even though this is counterintuitive as the material object would remain with us and is in our possession, it is somewhat like the economic term 'DIMINISHING MARGINAL UTILITY'. It means that the utility derived from the consumption of every additional unit of the same product diminishes, likewise there is no incremental happiness derived from the material objects after a certain point.

The 'HIGH' gained from objects are short-lived and thus with time the utility derived begins to decline or diminish. It seldom contributes to our long-term happiness. Ironically, the constant presence of the material possession makes it easier to adapt to and makes it less exciting. Nonetheless, when we make a sojourn to a tropical island, or enjoy a weekend hike, it gets etched in our memory and becomes a bigger part of our identity, while material possessions actually remain outside of us, just taking up space that we get accustomed to. **Ultimately, we are really the sum total of our experiences and not our possessions.**

Experiences are also invaluable as they form bonds and could also become reasons for animated discussions. They kindle associations and fire relationships with people around us. We are more likely to connect with someone because we took a vacation together to Greece; than we are to connect with someone because we bought them an expensive phone or watch.

People bond over experiences that they discuss. A discussion on the trek up the Himalayas is far more interesting as a topic of conversation than say the new 'curvy television' that we had bought.

Moreover, the phenomenon of "keeping up with the Jones" causes negative comparative bench marks. When we compare material things we realise that they do not contribute to our overall happiness in anyway.

Research done and published by Gilovich and Amit Kumar, in the academic journal of '*Experimental Social Psychology*', confirm these observations. It would hence be smart to allocate our limited resources towards experiencing new things than material possessions.

That's why we need to take that vacation and go out and spend time experiencing new things, rather than getting stuck with our *PlayStations* playing mindless games. We should maximize our happiness smartly.

Investing in people

The other important thing is investing in people. There was once a picture I saw in a publication. One side of the picture depicted hell and the other half portrayed heaven. Actually, there was virtually no difference between the two. Both sides had people dining at a table and being served with bowls of soup. Both halves of the pictures had diners who were given soup spoons with really long stems.

The difference however was that on the half portraying hell, the diners were busy trying to consume their soup using their long spoons and it was hell. It was painfully difficult and downright impossible to feed oneself. The long stems of the spoon made scooping the soup and eating it a nightmare and thus the people in hell were miserable and hungry. In the picture of heaven everything was the same. However, the diners instead of feeding themselves fed the person opposite to them and it was all harmony and sweet.

The allegory on the long spoons is a parable, a folklore that has become part of many cultures; Jewish, Hindu, Buddhist, Christian, and is narrated with variations. It speaks of people and our interdependence.

When we are selfish and we think only of self-gratification without acknowledging or recognising the other, we would only hurt ourselves and build misery and pain. It is here on earth that we could make our heaven when we empathise, learn to be considerate and think of our fellow beings.

To stand alone, as an island we would slowly perish without nourishment for our inner selves. However, when we build ties and real relationships, which are beyond mere courtesy, we would then build a sense of community that nurtures one another. Having a serving mentality and valuing your neighbour does have its paybacks to us as individuals and to society as a whole.

Chapter 7

LESS GREED, MORE PASSION,

Choose 'Financial Freedom' and NOT 'Financial Greedom'

Why you should set aside greed and live life according to your passions
"...not doing what we love in the name of greed
is very poor management of our lives."

- Warren Buffett

"Your time is limited,
so, don't waste it living someone else's life.
Don't be trapped by dogma – which is living with the results of other people's thinking.
Don't let the noise of others' opinions drown out your own inner voice.
And most important,
have the courage to follow your heart and intuition."

- Steve Jobs

No billionaire in the world is going to carry his/her bank balance or assets when his/her time is up. Everyone is equal in death. It always makes me wonder at the pointless score keeping, when one's life is much richer when looked at holistically.

The Result of 'Financial Greedom'

The famous work by Russian author Leo Tolstoy **'How much land does a man require?'** is apt for today's time. In that story a group of rich land lords, land owners known as Bashkirs tell a peasant named Pahom that for a thousand roubles he could have as much land as he wants. There was a catch though, Pahom had to circle the land he wanted and return to the starting point by sunset. He would only accrue the land which he could walk around from sunrise to sunset.

Pahom starts out at dawn and covered vast swathes of land running all through the day. He arrived at the starting point at dusk only to drop dead. He was then buried in a grave six feet in length, which ironically answered the question posed by the title of the short story by Leo Tolstoy. As simple as the story is, it carries the powerful message that greed burns and destroys our valuable and intangible possessions. In, turn it would also destroy us.

While money is a definite need as laid out in the chapter 'Why Finances are like 'Oxygen', too much greed for it could slowly kill off our intangible wealth; like our health, family relationships, friendships, our passions and ultimately our happiness. It is therefore important for us to take a step back and understand how much we really need and why we would need that much. This could provide us with a better perspective and would stop our blind pursuit of material possessions. The mindless pursuit of mere monetary wealth would not only limit our happiness, it could also harm us.

Following one's Passion

"A runner must run with dreams in his heart, not money in his pocket."

- *Emil Zatopek*

"I learned from a very young age that if I pursued the things that truly excited me that they would reward in more important ways, like happiness."

- *Brandon Boyd*

To feel complete, one definitely needs to find a calling. We are most happy in our purposeful journey that we set for ourselves. It is the most important thing we could do for ourselves to sustain our drive and happiness. Very often following one's passion may involve making some initial sacrifices.

Yet the rewards reaped, gives us a sense of achievement. The exhilaration gained from having accomplished something in terms of happiness and contentment would make the journey well worth it. To quote Ellen DeGeneres, ***"I say always follow your passion, no matter what, because even if it's not the same financial success, it'll lead you to the money that'll make you the happiest"***.

Once I was at a famous outlet dealing with electronic goods. The owner a hefty and relatively obese gentleman was seated near the cashier's desk monitoring all the cash transactions that were being made. He had been doing this for decades reporting to work right from his younger days until today. He made tons of money in the process, working long hours with very few days off. He was still at it accumulating wealth at an increasing pace.

However, his health was deteriorating at an equally rapid rate. He heaved and panted as he stood up to have a closer look at some of the transactions. He lost his temper at employees, who cowered in fright and helplessness. It made me wonder, why was he so glued into making money when what he should be doing is taking care of his health? Well, the answer was greed. It would have been best if he had considered other aspects of his life that would have made him holistically richer than just the accumulation of wealth.

Money can take us up to a certain point in life, beyond that the baton is to be handed over to better sense and passion to guide us through our lives. To quote Pablo Picasso **"Never permit a dichotomy to rule your life, a dichotomy in which you hate what you do so you can have pleasure in your spare time. Look for a situation in which your work will give you as much happiness as your spare time"**. Blessed are those who understand that and those who have the wherewithal to follow up on that. The rest of us would just trudge along, dragging our lives in a desert searching for that elusive oasis, hoping that it isn't a mirage that has been drawing us in endlessly.

Most people are in a rat race, running on the tread mill of life, too scared to get off. We need to ask honest questions to ourselves and by introspecting we could truly understand what we would really like to do. Of course, it is easier when we attain the threshold of 'Financial Freedom' and the first half of the book could help us accomplish that. We can and should dream.

Following our passion is our rightful path to happiness. Our responsibilities, our work have always made up for our time. Many of us who have attained financial freedom still fear making the change. It is important for us to introspect and to understand what is holding us back. This inner enquiry should be guided by our heart while the chatter around us should be ignored. We need to listen to our inner voice as it does have something to say about our aspirations and our intrinsic self-worth.

Conclusion

"Success is not the key to happiness. Happiness is the key to success. If you love what you are doing, you will be successful. "

- Albert Schweitzer

"I always was a rich person because money is not related to happiness."

- Paulo Coelho

One is rich not because one has a billion dollars, but because one has a billion dreams. Live your dreams when you can and do it now!! Drop greed and embrace your passions. One day when you do look back, you would feel complete and bask in the warm glow reflected from the rich, interesting and happy life lived.

So, fill your life with things you want to do. The Time is NOW!!

Chapter 8

SOCIETY AND CULTURE

How Technology and Economics are going to impact Society and Culture

"The decadent international but individualistic capitalism in the hands of which we found ourselves after the war is not a success. It is not intelligent. It is not beautiful. It is not just. It is not virtuous. And it doesn't deliver the goods."

- John Maynard Keynes

"Capitalism' is a dirty word for many intellectuals, but there are a number of studies showing that open economies and free trade are negatively correlated with genocide and war."

- Steven Pinker

Does economics affect the way society and cultures evolve? Does technology subtly affect the cultural moorings of a society? On cursory inspection the impact of economics and its major role in society and culture may not be apparent.

Environmental factors such as geography and climate, and factors such as economics and feasibility have dictated everything from food, clothing and housing in every society. This has resulted in the formation of unique cultures around the world.

Economics influences the evolution of society, for example agrarian societies are different from coastal societies and their merchant cultures.

While commerce and economics have been moulding and shaping civilization, technological change came in as a subtle influence that then brought about paradigm shifts in society and culture. These subtle influences then challenged traditional ways of doing things.

The impact of technology is undeniable.

Why Economics?

"Start with the idea that you can't repeal the laws of economics, even if they are inconvenient."

- Lawrence Summers

"Technology can create needs
even as it
addresses them."

- Andrew Yang

When *Coca Cola*, the famous soft drinks giant re-entered India after liberalisation of the Indian economy, Coca Cola's executive head was asked in an interview about how he planned on getting ahead of his competitor *Pepsi*.

The executive immediately said that his competition was not Pepsi but *nimbu-paani* (lemonade) and tender coconut water sold by small vendors. He was clear that his real competition was from the juice and refreshment vendors at every street corner.

Initially, the prices of both Coke and Pepsi were not competitive when compared to the fresh juices sold by street vendors. 250ml Coke sold for more than a serving of tender coconut water or *nimbu-paani*. However, with time, the cost of Coke and Pepsi when compared to traditional drinks dropped, while traditional natural drinks became more expensive.

This initially shot up the demand for soft drinks allowing them early traction in the market. Such is the power of economics.

However, as the middle class grew with greater purchasing power, they began to prefer healthier options, even at higher prices. This is why the soft drinks market in India will not reach its expected potential because nowadays most people have begun to prefer natural and healthier options.

World over natural juices and cold pressed juices are becoming more and more popular, even if the costs are steep. With consumer awareness, consumer behaviour shows that people are making healthier choices.

Thus, we are again going to see the re-emergence of the *juice-walas* who sell at every street corner. This shift in choice was only brought on by economics and changing priorities. The short-term cost of quenching thirst is weighed against the long-term healthcare costs of unhealthy drinks, and hence more and more people are making informed choices based on holistic thinking.

The Role of Economics

"I looked back on the roaring Twenties - with its jazz, 'Great Gatsby,' and the pre-Code films
- as a party I had somehow managed to miss.
After World War Two, I expected something similar, a return to the period after the first war,
but when the skirt lengths went down instead of up,
I knew we were in big trouble."

- Hugh Hefner

"In human life, economics precedes politics or culture."

- Park Geun- hye

As much as technology impacts society and culture, economics is the *'Tipping factor'*. The role of economics on society is not to be dismissed. It is sometimes the sole deciding factor. However, technology has a pivotal role to play in that it makes the economics possible by driving down the price of goods and services. In this way, new technologies get mainstream acceptance, once the trade-offs are just right.

Once new ways of doing things get into the consciousness of the people, society sees change. The new generations are often the early change agents. Whether it is the advent of radio, television, movies, cable television, direct to home or now OTT ('Over the Top' media streaming) services, these all have impacted and changed society and exposed us to varied cultures. Music cassettes, compact discs, *Mp3*, *walk-mans*, iPods, mobile phones, *blue-tooth* have over the years altered popular culture and imagination.

White goods, such as refrigerators, dish-washers, washing-machines, microwave ovens, cooking ranges etc., have provided convenience and saved time. These have also enabled the liberation of women who were then able to invest time in their careers and take on paid work. This has then led to gender equality and emancipation of women.

The internet and mobile phone services have caused an information explosion, impacting education, cross cultural exchanges, food habits and dressing styles. It has changed and has empowered millions. Social media and access to news has even helped people in repressed countries to protest and demand freedom. Social and environmental movements have gained traction and have impacted the way we think and behave.

One of the most impactful changes has been brought about by cheap data services provided by mobile carriers. It has democratised information and allowed the marginalised to access information and services. It has also helped governments reach out to people in all corners. Hopefully, this would lead to more equitability and fairness, where no one would be left behind.

In the future, with time, we are going to see the costs of education and healthcare drop. Not only is society going to become more aware of the marginalised, it is also going to get to the point where it will be able to guarantee minimum living standards to all people.

As we begin to enter the 'golden age' of human history, information and knowledge are going to be commodities while innovation and creativity are going to be highly valued and prized. While the marginalised have been caught in their struggle to fulfil day to day needs, the new age will bring about change and every one would have the opportunity to pursue and realise their full potential. When we enable all, we would be able to tackle all problems facing us and unlock the massive human potential that has been wasted in the past.

While human ingenuity can be trusted to find solutions to our most pressing problems, human nature could prove to be our Achilles heel. However, if guided by wisdom we could prevent our self-destruction and rise above petty differences to achieve prosperity and happiness for all. In this context, wisdom is more important than intelligence.

The Revolutionary Milestones in Societal Evolution

"Human society has dense borders - economic, religious and cultural - inculcated from an early age. We hate change."

- Alejandro Jodorowsky

"We inhabit an obscure planet, in an obscure galaxy, around an obscure sun, but on the other hand, modern human society represents one of the most complex things we know."

- David Christian

Technological progress has changed the economic standards of people around the world for centuries. With better economic prospects and time freed up for activities beyond work, lifestyles have undergone vast changes. Society has been impacted and even cultural aspects have seen adaptations and change.

Agricultural Revolution

When agriculture first took root, civilisation began. Families were nurtured and population began to grow steadily as more tracts of farm land came under the plough. Economic growth corresponded to the increase in population. As larger families worked the land, production increased but this was offset by more mouths to feed. This also meant that per capita growth was stagnant. This revolution was the first agricultural revolution which laid the foundation for civilization.

Industrial Revolution

Once the industrial revolution took hold with mass production, large quantities of goods were produced. As efficiencies increased, goods became affordable. Incremental innovation and newer technologies helped to create big shifts. This contributed greatly in increased production and affordability of the produced goods. In the industrialised and developed countries this helped spawn the middle class, who catalysed this revolution and were at the fore front it. Even still, the vast majority of people worked hard to make ends meet and to put food on the table. The generation of workers during the Industrial revolution toiled long hours to sustain a roof over their head and provide for their families. This generation worked for their needs.

Computer Revolution

However, as technology leapfrogged and with the coming of the electronic and computer age, productivity multiplied and provided workers with much improved wages and quality of life. While electronic and white goods made life easier freeing up time for work and leisure, entire new verticals and industries grew. Computers enhanced productivity and there was a quantum leap in the efficiency of many sectors. Industries were able to manage their production activities, material and human resources in a more efficient and effective manner. Across industries higher wages and more affordable products meant workers were no more working for sustenance but were now working for a standard of living. This was the generation of the IT (Information Technology) revolution.

MIS (Mobile, Internet and Social) Revolution

Gradually, with the internet age and the advent of the smart phone a new era germinated. The great increases in productivity enabled by explosive innovation over decades meant that this generation would come into an era where they would be paid remuneration that would be beyond just sustenance or standard of living. This generation is in the midst of the social revolution where work life balance is central and priorities beyond money matter. This generation has different needs. It is hyper connected and every moment in one's life is shared, celebrated and broadcast, making each person a mini celebrity. This generation is sensitive to the image they showcase and have the luxury of work life balance and great pay. It is a generation that has numerous choices and styles of living they could choose from and afford. This revolution has showered the generation with a surfeit of life choices.

AI Revolution

The next generation though is going to be born in the midst of the AI (Artificial Intelligence) revolution where most mundane work is going to be taken over by machines. Work weeks are going to shrink further and may be as little as 12 hours a week. This generation is going to live with not just a high standard of living but are also going to be able to pursue their passions beyond work.

On the bedrock of decades of work done by the previous generations, this generation is going to enjoy the complete fulfilment of their dreams. It is going to be a future where time, money, tools and opportunity are all going to come together opening the door to phenomenal possibilities

The generation is going to be able to live life on its terms and achieve great pinnacles. Their limitations would only be personal and they wouldn't need to overcome much of the economic and social barriers that have held back generations of the past.

To rephrase the words of Oprah Winfrey it would be an age where truly one's attitude would be the only limitation to one's altitude.

Conclusion

No society or culture around the world has been left untouched by technological change. Within generations, societies adapt to the change. Cultures gradually soften and bend to accommodate the new needs, desires and aspirations of the younger generation.

However resistant one may be, change is ultimately inevitable. It is easier for societies to accommodate and move along with the change than to try and repel it.

Often change is for the better, and if not, society will outgrow that change anyway. So, there is nothing to doubt or fear. Embrace and ride the waves of change coming your way.

With a little flexibility and fluid thinking, one would be able to adapt and reap benefits of these waves.

So, raise your sails and enjoy the ride!

Chapter 9

FUTURE OF 'WEALTH'

What will 'Future Wealth' look like?

"Empty pockets never held anyone back.
Only empty heads and empty hearts can do that."

- Norman Vincent Peale

"Wealth is the ability
to
fully experience life."

- Henry David Thoreau

Early Wealth

The early wealth of humans who were 'hunters and gatherers' was related to the environment in which they functioned. As they began to rear cattle, horses, hens, goats and sheep, wealth began to be measured by the number of cattle they owned.

The early humans were nomadic and wandered from pasture to pasture feeding and taking care of their domesticated stock. Wealth in those times came to be measured by the count of domesticated stock in one's possession.

It is pretty interesting to note that even today in many parts of the world cattle wealth is taken as a serious barometer of personal wealth and status. In parts of Africa and India, a person is introduced as an owner of such and such number of domesticated cattle. In fact, in this day and age the practice of gifting a set number of cattle as dowry in marriage still prevails in quite a few places.

The advent of agriculture spurred human settlements and land soon became a resource. Land was fenced and ownership of land and homes became possible and necessary. Wealth began to be measured in terms of acres of land held along with the count of domesticated livestock.

Land even today holds great importance and many people including the likes of the current richest man in the world today, *Jeff Bezos*, all hold large tracts of land. In fact, Bezos is rumoured to have one of the largest land holdings in the US to his name.

Real estate in the form of land has and will always be a kind of wealth that humans value because it is a piece of this limited earth. However, its value relative to other forms of wealth has and will continue to undergo sea changes moving it up and often down the pecking order in comparison to newer forms of wealth.

Gold and the beginning of 'Modern Banking'

Gold has been a wealth barometer for some centuries now and it simultaneously took root as a currency across many different civilizations, as gold began to be used in barter and trade. As a currency it is highly valued for its consistent appearance, aesthetic qualities, rarity, durability and malleability.

Gold treasures belonging to ancient Thracians dating back to as far as 5th millennium B.C. have been found in *Varna Necropolis* in Bulgaria. In 3100 B.C., the Egyptian ruler *Menes* laid the foundation for incorporating gold into the Egyptian economy and had decreed that "one part of gold in value was equal to 2.5 parts of silver".

Gold was also an integral part of the *Indus Valley civilization* in India and was used in jewellery and as barter.

The first official declaration of gold as money came in 600 B.C. when *King Alyattes* of *Lydia* oversaw the first recorded mint. Coins which were an alloy of gold and silver called electrum were stamped with denominations. *Darius I* of Persia introduced a 95.83% pure 8.4g gold coin minted from his treasury, which was deemed equivalent to 20 silver coins.

Roman Society which had been using coins for exchange also introduced gold coins in 300 B.C. and this was continued by the *Byzantine Empire* until the middle-ages. The Italian *Florin* became the most dominant gold coin along with the German *Augustalis* introduced under *Frederick II*. By the 14th century England had also moved towards using gold as a currency by minting its coins known as *Noble*.

Unsurprisingly, most treasures in the world involved gold. One famous surviving treasure vault was discovered at the famed *Shree Padmanabhaswamy Temple* in Thiruvananthapuram, Kerala, India. The vaults of the temple are rumoured to hold an estimated Rs. 1 trillion (US $20 Billion) of wealth in gold and other precious commodities in just one of its many vaults. The *'Vault-B'* of the temple was opened and audited under the aegis of the Supreme Court of India and unimaginable wealth in the form of gold coins and necklaces were discovered inside.

Apart from being a part of treasures around the world, gold also helped to kick start the first banking system. The fractional banking system first took hold in England after goldsmiths started to re-lend gold that had been deposited with them for storage in lieu of receipts in the early gold markets.

The confiscation of large amounts of gold as forced loan by *King Charles I* led to many merchants storing gold with the gold smiths. This was the genesis of the 'fractional banking system'. As a convenience and for the safety of the gold traded, the system would circulate the titles of ownership of gold rather than the gold itself.

In the year 1816, the UK officially defined the pound sterling relative to gold. With the entry of the United States of America, the 'classic' gold standard was adopted in 1879 and was further solidified in 1900.

The *Bretton-woods agreement* signed in 1944 laid the foundation for convertible currencies where countries settled their international balances in dollars and the US dollar became fully convertible to gold. The exchange rate applied at that time was $35/ounce which was the responsibility of the United States.

While the major powers constantly undermined the gold standard it was not until 1971 that the Federal government in the United States jettisoned the 'gold standard' once and for all. From then on it was the dollar trade that became the central theme of global trade and the 'US dollar' became established as the standard and preferred currency for trade.

Wealth Redefined

"If money is your hope for independence, you will never have it. The only real security that a man will have in this world is a reserve of knowledge, experience, and ability"

- Henry Ford

While 'cattle', 'land' and 'gold' were initial bedrocks of wealth. The industrial revolution created new forms of wealth. Industrialization brought on rapid growth, mass production of goods, large scale factories with a large workforce. These not only created jobs but also created multi-millionaires and billionaires who amassed unimaginable wealth.

A factory may only require small acreages but it had the capacity to churn out goods that got traded far and wide, making its owners unimaginably rich and powerful. The first few factories produced products including agricultural items, textiles, and machine parts.

The invention of the assembly line famously pioneered by Ford, manufactured and assembled goods. For those days, the output production rates were phenomenal.

Vast amounts of wealth were created in the process and wealth began to be redefined. One was wealthy not just by owning vast tracks of land and gold, ownership of companies that managed factories and supply chains and other such avenues, also created wealth.

Andrew Carnegie was the richest person in the world at a time when wealth was amassed from production and selling of factory goods. He amassed his wealth namely from his vertically integrated iron and steel business where he owned the entire supply chain from the mines to the railroads and controlled the pricing of the end product.

Unlocking of Wealth and 'Paper Money'

The *'East India Company'* became the first publicly traded company in the world. Trading across the globe was very risky as ships could get lost or destroyed in storms, or have its load plundered by pirates and many a time it may suffer mutinies. These risks were too many for one investor to withstand and it was but natural that the 'East India Company' was formed to spread the risk and rewards of its endeavours.

Thus, it became the first limited liability company. It was formed in the year 1600 A.D and was called *'Governor and Company of Merchants of London trading with the East Indies'*. This helped to diversify risk and mitigate it, as its investments were spread over a number of voyages. This reduced risk and chance of catastrophic failure if investments in a particular voyage drew a blank. In the year 1602 A.D., the first shares of the 'East India Company' were released in the *Amsterdam stock exchange*.

While the *New York Stock Exchange (NYSE)* was formed in 1817 A.D., the *NASDAQ* was created in the year 1971 A.D. Since then, a number of stock exchanges have been created in a number of countries around the world. Large amounts of wealth today reside in these stock exchanges as paper money. A number of entrepreneurs have listed their businesses in the stock markets of the world and they dominate the Forbes list of richest people in the world.

The Oil Economy

The initial demand for oil was satisfied by hunting whales and extracting oil from its blubber by flensing. This became a major occupation across Europe, United States and many countries in East Asia. The Whaling industry reached its peak during the latter half of the 18th century. In fact, whale hunting was a significant part of the GDP of many countries during that time.

The discovery and production of oil from drilling and the ability to extract kerosene from coal, caused the whaling industry to wane. Until, the signing of 'The International Convention for the Regulation of Whaling', whale hunting continued. The convention not only brought on international action to prohibit and discourage the hunting of whales but also spoke of conservation of whale stock.

Ever since the industrial revolution, the demand for coal and oil has grown exponentially and businesses involved in the extraction of coal/oil, have and continue to mint a lot of money. Initially, the 'Carbon Economy' was defined by coal mining. The demand for kerosene and gasoline has been growing ever since the automobile revolution.

Right from the industrial revolution to the information revolution, the 'Carbon Economy' as it is called, has defined wealth in the 20th century right into the 21st century.

The rise of personal transport and global trade with automobiles and gasoline/diesel powered transport has caused the oil economy to peak and with time find new peaks. In the 19th century, *J.D.Rockefeller Sr.* controlled 90% of the oil economy in the United States. At one point this made him the richest American until he was surpassed by Andrew Carnegie. Wealth lay rooted in the 'Carbon Economy' ever since.

The 'Carbon Economy' and the industrial dependence on fuel spurred the rise and growth of a number of countries especially those in the Middle-East. These countries were endowed with vast quantities of natural wealth constituted by oil and gas. Due to the voracious demands of the 'Carbon Economy' their resources were much valued and were in great demand. Oil defined wealth and continues to do so.

However, headwinds have begun to appear as there is talk that the 'Carbon Economy' would give way to 'Renewable Energy Economy' with the advent of Electric Vehicles and Solar power. Just as IC engines and thermal power plants defined the 20th Century, these new technologies that use renewable energy would define the 21st century.

The Computer and Chip revolution

Talking about sources of wealth, the 20th Century has seen the rise of computers and faster chips. Sources of 'Intangible wealth' beyond just tangible products or traded commodities began to become significant. This has caused a paradigm shift in the way wealth is built and measured. Software codes were written to power the hardware, and its usefulness has led to its rise as a source of intangible wealth.

Microsoft, a company that envisioned a PC on every desktop foresaw that its operating system would be running on every computer. It became one of the world's most sought-after stocks in the late 20th century. Hardware companies such as Intel grew in tandem producing faster and faster microprocessors to power the ever-increasing demand of software upgrades. Wealth in the late 20th century and even today lay in these intangibles. These teeny-weenie wealth creating chips, are certainly far removed from wealth constituted by land and gold of yesteryears.

The Information Superhighway

The coming of the 'internet' or the 'information superhighway' simply began a revolution that spawned hundred others. The internet and flow of information provided the basis for smart entrepreneurs to reach out to markets, offer services, control supply chains, outsource manufacturing, market to consumers, take-in e-payments in a manner never seen before.

A staggering number of businesses riding on the back of the internet were born and many continue to flourish even as new businesses with newer business models come into vogue.

The information Superhighway provided the basis for 'Creative Destruction' at its best. Giants like '*Amazon*' and '*Google*' were born and have created new kinds of wealth. These companies have provided customers with tools to find exactly what they want and give them access to ways to fulfil their needs.

There has been a tectonic shift as flow of information has increased efficiency of supply chains, opened new markets, increased convenience to customers, enabled targeted marketing and has even changed the way that people live their lives. This new wealth redefined the way money was seen since the late 20th Century.

The Mobile Revolution

The smart phone revolution is however the real game changer. Taking off from the feature phone, the smart phone is a powerful computing device in a customer's hand constantly relaying information 'back and forth' to company servers via a variety of applications called 'Apps'.

This has not only created new avenues to serve the customer but has made the computing device omnipresent and omnipotent.

The customers can now hail a cab, lookup restaurants, order food delivery, shop, play games, pay and chat all through one device in his/her pocket.

There is a paradigm shift where customisation and in-depth customer information allowed one to cater more specifically and effectively to the customer's needs. New models for delivery of services and new models to reach out to each individual consumer, to get their attention, time and money, are affected by these technologies.

These are new ways of reaching out and fulfilling business motives. This is the new reality. Wealth has been created by taking a number of businesses right into a device in the hands of the consumer.

Social Media revolution

It would be pertinent to mention the 'Social Media' revolution in this context. The 'Social Media' companies allow the consumer to use their services for free and in exchange they obtain the personal data of the consumers.

These companies also own all posted data and comb them to understand the profile of the consumers and provide them with tailor made services. Better understanding of the customers would mean better targeted advertisements.

Such services are invaluable to advertisers, product and service providers around the world. Rather than the 'spray and pray' advertising of the past, targeting occurs at a micro level and each of the customers can be individually and effectively marketed to.

Any manufacturer or service provider could define his/her target market and these social media channels would be invaluable channel partners to reach out to the customers with their marketing messages.

These manufacturing and service companies are willing to pay big dollars to anyone who helps them to sell more. That is how 'Social Media' giants rake in the *moolah*, sometimes cents at a time for every target that they connect with.

Like little drops make an ocean, when we consider the extent of their global networks and number of users, these cents per click translates into billions of dollars in revenue.

Data the 'New Oil'

Consequently, data has now become the 'new oil'. It has become the resource that companies seek to harness to be able to understand and to better serve their customers. Companies seem bent on gathering this data and deep mining it for insights to be able to sell better to their customer.

Companies on social media like *Facebook, LinkedIn, WhatsApp, Instagram, Twitter* etc., sit on a treasure trove of data that can be mined for a variety of new applications and services.

With IoT (Internet of Things) and AI (Artificial Intelligence) taking centre stage in the 21st century, we are at the helm of an age where large quantities of data will be available and exploited. In this regard the "raw material" is DATA.

Companies are in a race to gather as much of this gold as possible. It significantly matters who owns the data and who has access to it. The entire wealth of the new age companies resides on 'server farms' in the form of this data.

AI requires huge amounts of data to feed bots and enable machine learning. This aids machine response to new situations as and when they arise. The *Google's* Self-Driving Car for instance has recorded over 1.5 million miles of testing providing invaluable insights that could help train the self-driving software to respond to the varied situations it may confront in the future.

The learning is such that it may be able to respond to situations it may not have confronted in the past. These kinds of insights that help in training an AI system however need vast amounts of data.

Another example is healthcare. As 'wearables' become a rage, and as more and more data are collected from the devices that people wear, greater insights can be obtained to make these devices more accurate and also to break new ground in the fitness and health segment. Hence it does not come as a surprise that bits of data on servers is the new wealth or as some call it, the 'new oil'.

As a civilization that measured wealth by literally counting sheep and livestock we have come a long way. Today bits and bytes of information are a major source of wealth and going forward as the world becomes richer it can be hoped that people may move towards a more holistic definition of wealth as defined at an individual level. Some call this the 'True Wealth'.

'True' Wealth

Philosophically speaking real wealth is more than just money. In the simplest terms 'True Wealth' is the ability to live life on one's own terms. It's freedom to have and exercise choices.

Individually speaking there are different kinds of wealth.

You can be wealthy in….

- Money & Possessions (Financial Wealth)
- Fame & Fortune
- Health & Happiness (Health Wealth)
- Purpose & Direction in Life
- Family & Friends (Relationship Wealth)
- Love & Laughter
- Freedom & Time (Time Wealth)
- Talent & Wisdom (Wealth of Wisdom)
- Peace of Mind & Spirituality (Spiritual Wealth)

As people move up the economic ladder, wealth as defined by money has diminishing rates of return and people look beyond it. People in many developed nations are valuing fewer working hours and more family time.

More and more people are beginning to believe that blind consumption with disregard to the environment would only hurt the planet and come back to bite us as a race. Movements to work and care for the environment are growing. People have begun to believe that environmental health is true wealth we could leave for the future generations.

There is also greater awareness among the new generation to stay healthy. The shift towards vegetarianism and veganism is an example of how people are making better choices to not just safeguard the environment but also to take care of their health.

Healthy environment and healthy living are maxims that people are swearing by today. They choose organic food and prefer sustainable agriculture.

More and more people are taking their health and fitness seriously. This only goes to show that wealth has many dimensions. 'Health is wealth' goes an old adage and the new generation have made an early start. The world is moving towards holistic living where they value physical fitness and living a stress-free life. In this context it would be pertinent to mention how popular *Yoga* has become.

Individual wealth seen through the prism of 'True Wealth' is a function of our environment, the food we consume, the water we drink and the air we breathe. These need to be healthy just like our immediate living environment.

These are part of our 'True wealth'. This 'True Wealth' will be affected by our lifestyle and the choices we make.

How we consume and how we discard what we don't need, all make up our *carbon foot print* and could build or break our future. As inheritors of the planet, the future generations are more attuned towards the need to save the environment.

We have come a long way and we are on a path where our views and perceptions about wealth will change to include that which makes holistic and sustainable living possible.

As the world becomes wealthier, wealth will begin to be seen beyond just GDP and per capita income. The true physical, mental, spiritual health of the population will be seen as a measure of true wealth.

GDH or *Gross domestic happiness* as a central measure will take hold once the world has been through this mindless and soulless materialism cycle. This will happen gradually with greater realisation.

'True wealth' seen holistically has begun to see the dawn. With greater realisation in this century there is going to be a fundamental shift in what basically contributes to and constitutes wealth. The traditional definitions of wealth are going to undergo a major overhaul once again!

Chapter 10

VIBRATIONS AND THE UNIVERSE

Why every 'Small Vibration' Matters

"If you want to find the secrets of the universe,
think in terms of
energy, frequency and vibration."

- Nikola Tesla

"Every moment there are a million miracles happening around you:
a flower blossoming,
a bird tweeting,
a bee humming,
a raindrop falling,
a snowflake wafting along the clear evening air.
There is magic everywhere.
If you learn how to live it,
life is nothing short of a daily miracle."

- Sadhguru

It is interesting that in *Sanatana Dharma*, Lord *Shiva* is shown with a ***Damaru*** in his hand. The *Damaru* is a two-sided small drum that fits into his hand.

Lord *Shiva* in this depiction is seen to be playing the *Damaru,* as he sends out the spiritual vibrations. These Spiritual Vibrations are used to create and regulate the Universe.

While these may seem as a Spiritual depiction or even Mumbo Jumbo (to the uninformed), it will be prudent to note that this has some deeper meaning and truth to it.

The Universe right from the dawn of creation, which we may say is the BIG BANG starting from a single point and expanding to form the visible universe as we see it today, consists of nothing but these vibrations.

ATOMS and WHAT THEY CONTAIN

"The best armour of old age is
a well-spent life
preceding it."

- *Charlie Munger*

"Love is your quality.
Love is not what you do.
Love is what you are."

- *Sadhguru*

In the Scientific World when atoms (*Anu* as described in early Sanskrit Verses) were observed at a very small granular level it was found to contain Electrons, Protons and Neutrons.

However, what is interesting is that when observed even more deeply 99% of an atom is just actually empty space and what we have are just vibrations happening at a very minute granular level.

In fact, we are nothing but made up of these zillion small vibrations.

Where PHYSICS meets PHILOSOPHY

"Act only according to that maxim
whereby you can, at the same time,
will that it should
become a universal law."

- Kant

"Happiness is
NOT based
on
achievements.
It's an attitude, cultivated by appreciating the simple things in life
and
valuing relationships over possessions."

- Gaur Gopal Das

In fact, the entire UNIVERSE is nothing but predominantly energy in the form of these vibrations, which are powered by the zillions and zillions of these small vibrations.

Mass are just knots in these fields of energy. Mass can be seen as concentration of energy at points in space. While all mass in the world is ultimately an aggregate of these small vibrations, the difference between inanimate and animate objects is 'consciousness' or *Chit* as in ancient Sanskrit texts.

The Chit or consciousness allows us to modify or regulate our integrity framework of the aggregate small vibrations that constitute ourselves. These aggregate vibrations tend to draw similar vibrations and help us grow our collective destiny.

Physicist Albert Einstein, did propose the 'Theory of Relativity'. However, at an atomic level, the theory failed to capture what was happening.

The laws of 'Quantum Mechanics' provided a more reliable basis to explain mass and energy at an atomic level. Since then, Physicists are still looking for a theory that would bring the 'Theory of Relativity' and 'Theory of Quantum Mechanics' on a common platform.

A platform that is often referred to as the 'The UNIFIED THEORY of EVERYTHING'.

Science has found that LIGHT PHOTONs for instance can behave BOTH like a PARTICLE and a WAVE. Further theories such as ENTANGLEMENT and STRING THEORY have left Physicists baffled and more confused.

Also, a UNIFIED theory that connects the 'Theory of Relativity' with 'Quantum Mechanics' has still been elusive to scientists.

However, if we begin to see the UNIVERSE as made up of Zillion vibrations with 'Mass and Energy' being just different manifestations of these vibrations, we may just begin to see the connections leading to a UNIFIED THEORY of EVERYTHING.

Ultimately, Both MASS and ENERGY are made up of zillions of these small vibrations and are just different manifestations of these vibrations.

It can be imagined and said that when a bunching or grouping of these vibrations occur within an integrity framework, particular manifestations of energy and mass comes into being.

Mass is just concentrated knots in energy fields.

BOTH Energy and Mass, are fundamentally just made up of small vibrations at the minutest of levels. Each grouping retains their respective integrity frameworks, with the essential integrity framework being unique to the grouping that governs them.

Interestingly, Mass and Energy are ultimately interchangeable. We can move Mass and Energy interchangeably from one integrity framework to the other.

UNIVERSAL VIBRATIONS

"What you do makes a difference,
and you have
to decide
what kind of difference you want to make"

-Jane Goodall

"The most beautiful moments in life are moments
when you are expressing your joy,
NOT when
you are seeking it."

- Sadhguru

Every Universe (among the ones in the infinite 'Alternative Universes') interestingly has a Certain Vibration as central to its Integrity framework. Within the Universe there are many stars and galaxies with their own vibrations. The 'sum of parts' however, make up the whole.

Interestingly EACH and EVERY human being has a SMALL VIBRATION in him. In various forms of Religion or Philosophies these are referred to as the SOUL. It is NOT just individuals that have a SOUL but so do all particles that make up the UNIVERSE in our reality.

However, humans have consciousness, which allows for them to shape these vibrations. Ultimately, these Vibrations do and can change. We are made up of Zillions of atoms having their own small vibrations which can respond to change originating within.

At an Individual level, all of us have an 'integrity framework'. When we move in directions that are NOT in sync with it, our inner vibrations will feel torn in different directions.

The point I am making is that if our actions are driven by LOVE and a CONCERN for each other we will create a VIBRATION framework for us on EARTH that will send out the VIBRATIONs of love. This would for instance attract other POSITIVE nurturing frameworks in our immediate environment and in our UNIVERSE.

For example, at the extreme level, the vibrations we send out as a planet will attract other aliens who have the SAME TYPE of Vibrations. This may lead to collaboration or destruction, depending on WHO we end-up attracting. This in turn is a function of our aggregate vibrations as a human species.

On the other hand, if our actions are driven by HATE and DESTRUCTION, we may end up with collective vibrations that may cause the end of humanity.

For instance, if we are driven by hate, we are likely to attract aliens who are also driven by hate. On the other hand, we may also end-up self-destructing.

Ironically the Universe would actually help and facilitate us to do what we want, including self-destruction, if that is what is our predominant aggregate vibrations are.

The Universe gives us what we ask for as a species.

If we choose LOVE we will survive and thrive, while if we choose HATE we will get exactly that, and end up destroying each other. Progress and technological development only serve to AMPLIFY our innate inner vibrations.

A society, civilization or species gets what it asks for and what it deserves. The only rules that matter, are those of the 'KARMIC balance of the UNIVERSE'. That balance gets restored at the appropriate time, no matter what.

The point is, 'The Universe does NOT care for HUMANS in particular'. There is really no privileged position assigned to humans in particular in the Universe.

This may stem from our temporary dominance and consequent arrogance born out of that position of dominance. While we need the Universe to exist, the universe does not need us to survive.

The status of superiority that humans assign themselves is just our delusion. Just as much as we thought we were the center of the Universe for thousands of years, until Copernicus and then Galileo came along (in Western* historical context).

(*The Indian civilization had long known and accepted that the 'earth was round' and that all 'planets revolved around the Sun'.

The Indian mathematician & astronomer ***Aryabhata*** had laid out that, the earth was round and that it was Helio-centric (that it revolved around the sun) in his works including *Arya-Siddhanta* and *Arya-bhatiya*, compiled in about 499 A.D.)

Hence, we can nurture ourselves and care for each other or go ahead hate and destroy each other. The fact, is the Universe does not care.

The Universe has its laws and cares about only maintaining the **Karmic Balances**. We choose and are responsible for our own collective fate.

For instance, there are Nuclear-weapons and AI. If humanity cannot develop an INTEGRITY framework of TRUST built on concern for fellow human beings, it is NOT difficult to see where this would end.

Both Nuclear-weapons and AI are examples of Technology that could AMPLIFY our CORE VIBRATIONS of HATE or LOVE. Choice is ours as Humanity. Universe is just a facilitator.

The Onus is on us as an intelligent specie to make sure that in our greed and rush, our SUPREME INTELLIGENCE does NOT get ahead of our COLLECTIVE WISDOM.

DIMENSIONs of the PROBLEM

"Life can only be understood backwards;
but it
must be lived forwards."

- Kierkegaard

"Too many people are hungry, not because there is a dearth of food.
It is because there is a dearth of love and care in human hearts."

- Sadhguru

"The day the power of love
overrules the
love of power,
the world will know peace."

- Mahatma Gandhi

The sobering thought is that the power we wield today is nothing compared to what is going to be in our hands going forward. It would be imperative that we humans base our work on LOVE. We need to develop an INTEGRITY FRAMEWORK which will be nurturing and caring, rather than on mistrust and hatred.

Tools of Science and Technology we have today alone are enough to destroy the Human race many times over. As we go forward, we are going to see potential for 'Amplified Outcomes' at levels we can't even phantom today.

Now the question is WITH WHAT are we going to SEED the future? WHAT are we going to teach and pass on to our children? The SEED we plant today, whether LOVE or HATE will determine our future and the future of our children. The choice is before us and we have the power to shape our COLLECTIVE DESTINY.

The most frightening part is that if we do not get our foundations right, and do it right now, we may end up moving forward with HATE in our hearts. 'HATE and GREED' in our hearts is guaranteed to make us all perish and die, as we hurtle towards SUCH a collective destiny.

A society or civilization GETS, what it DESERVES.

If we choose hate, the way the Universe works is that it will give us exactly what we ask for. It is just that this will be at ANOTHER LEVEL. If you consider how technology can amplify HATE or LOVE, it becomes clear why.

For instance, take atomic weapons. (which was described as 'harnessing the power' of the 'Creation of the Universe' by US President *Franklin D.Roosevelt*). Humans discovered that a small amount of mass can be converted to huge amounts of energy. The same tech can be used for destruction or to generate energy, we had and have a choice.

The Atomic weapon was really a 1st generation weapon. We then went on to develop the 2nd generation weapon, the Thermo-nuclear weapon. Now, we all know how destructive that can be.

The 2nd Generation 'Thermo-nuclear weapon' is on an exponential curve when compared to the 1st Generation 'Atomic weapon'. Now if I told that, we had barely begun to get started and it is possible to have a 9th Generation weapon. What would your reaction be?

You read right, 9th Generation weapon.

For one moment here, let us step back and take a deep breath, as we begin to grasp the magnitude of that kind of weapon. Each Generation of Weapon can pack a punch that is exponentially greater than the punch of the previous one.

A 9th generation weapon when setoff will be so powerful that it would end OUR UNIVERSE (This UNIVERSE being our reality in the multitude of ALTERNATIVE UNIVERSES). Such a weapon, when set-off would simply cause a REVERSE BIG BANG. It would bring our Universe back to a SINGLE POINT. Well, that is what 'HATE WHEN AMPLIFIED' looks like.

So, we have a Choice as our intelligence is directed to produce bigger and more powerful technology which consequently hands us the power to NURTURE or DESTROY ourselves.

All this starts with that SMALL VIBRATION in EACH ONE of us. Are we going to choose nurturing qualities of LOVE, UNDERSTANDING and EMPATHY, or are we going to let HATE be dominant and what those little vibrations are all about?

Even as we interact in this world, those small vibrations in us together are being collectively transmitted outwards and into the UNIVERSE. While Good Vibrations attract positive forces, Bad Vibrations attract negative forces.

Every day we are making choices that strengthen either the LOVE or HATE in us. It transmits outside, amplifies and seeks similar vibrations and then comes back to us many times over. PROGRESS in TECHNOLOGY just facilitates the amplification of our 'inner' little vibrations. A simple example is SOCIAL MEDIA. It helps us to sit and type on a keyboard and amplify our hate or love as it appears on screens of millions, who in turn respond. Technology can amplify our qualities as human beings whether good or bad, the choice is ours.

Honestly, the UNIVERSE DOES NOT CARE. It is ONLY programmed to give us what we desire as a human race.

Whether we send out LOVE or HATE from our individual hearts, we get back the same just at higher concentrations. As the saying goes, "What GOES around, DOES come around".

So, WHAT is that SMALL VIBRATION in our hearts going to be.

LOVE or HATE. Choice is Yours!

CONCLUDING FOOTNOTE

It is also hoped that 'The G-Forces' would be a useful read for administrators and act as a 'HANDBOOK for Policy-makers'. It is hoped that it could lend its' bit in helping Administrators to enhance their outlook, leading to holistic decision making.

It is hoped that 'THE G-FORCES' would be informative to administrators and be a foundation for actionable insights and for viewing issues with a fresh perspective. It is hoped that this book could benefit leaders (across the board) apart from policy makers and administrators.

Net-on-net it is hoped that this book would benefit society, while leading to ENHANCED POSITIVE OUTCOMES for society and humanity at a greater level.

Signing off for Now!

- A. Venkatasubramanian

ABOUT THE AUTHOR

Mr. **A.Venkatasubramanian a.k.a. 'A.V.'** has **authored 13 books,** including **'9 Non-Fiction Books'** and **'2 on Poetry and Songs'**. He has also **penned several articles** that were **published online** and **featured in newspaper columns.**

Mr. A.Venkatasubramanian is an **engineer** and **management graduate,** having done his **B.E.** from **India,** his **M.S. in Engineering** and **M.B.A. in General Management** and **Finance** from the **US**. He has also completed **CFA (Chartered Financial Analyst, USA)** until **Level II.**

While he made a start to his career in the **technology industry,** his experience spans a number of industries, including **automobiles, airlines, information technology, retail, banking, market research, real estate** and **finance.**

Mr. A.Venkatasubramanian is currently an **entrepreneur** in the **technology space** and loves **travel, photography, music** and the **arts.** He is an **avid reader** and **enjoys sports.**

SOCIAL MEDIA Links

PUBLICATIONS

100% of 'AUTHOR EARNINGS' Go to CHARITY

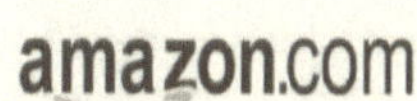

PUBLICATIONS
100% of 'AUTHOR EARNINGS' Go to CHARITY

Real Estate

Investing & Real Estate

Finance & Philosophy

Technology & Society

Entrepreneurship

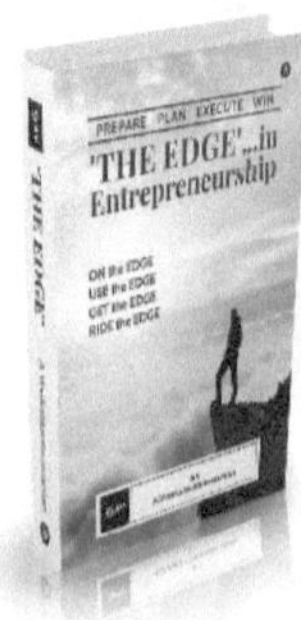

PUBLICATIONS
100% of 'AUTHOR EARNINGS' Go to CHARITY

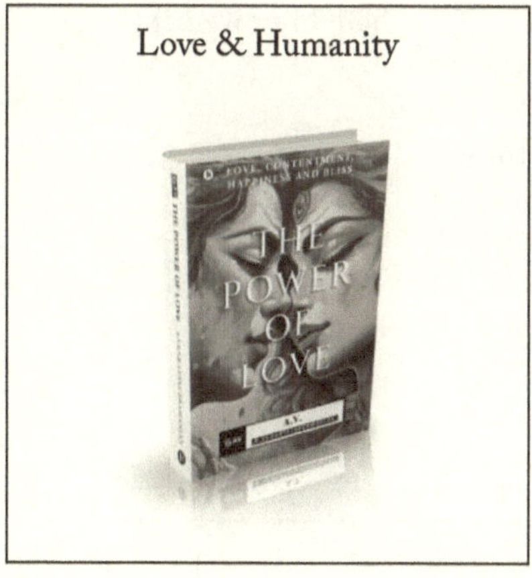

PUBLICATIONS
100% of 'AUTHOR EARNINGS' Go to CHARITY

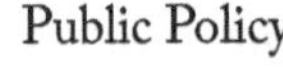
Public Policy

Administrator's Hand Book

Self-Improvement

PUBLICATIONS
100% of 'AUTHOR EARNINGS' Go to CHARITY

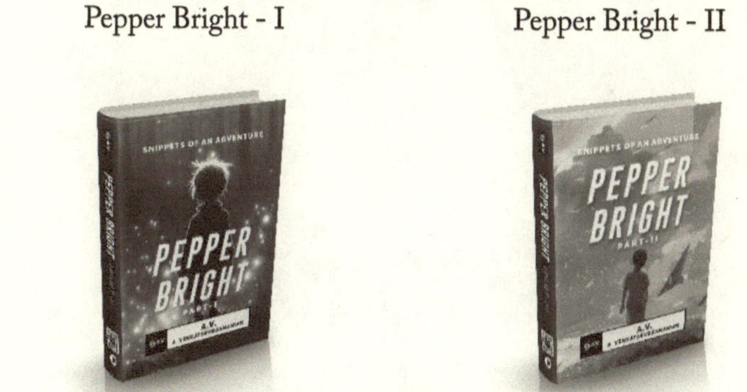

Pepper Bright - I

Pepper Bright - II

@

YouTube

Find us on YouTube

@

 **(AIR)**	 (AIM)	(AID)
Aastra Impact Records	Aastra Impact Media	Aastra Impact Dreams
	 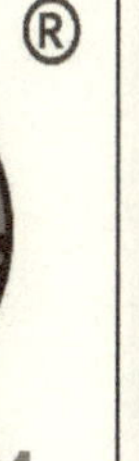	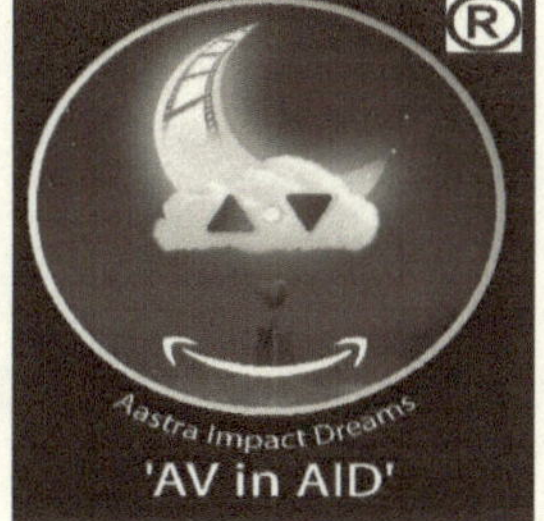

@	@	@

100% of Author's Earnings Go to Charity	100% of Author's Earnings Go to Charity	100% of Author's Earnings Go to Charity

@

Linkedin

Find us on Linkedin

Linkedin

@

<table>
<tr>
<td>

(AIR)

Aastra Impact Records

@

100% of Author's Earnings

Go to Charity

</td>
<td>

(AIM)

Aastra Impact Media

@

100% of Author's Earnings

Go to Charity

</td>
<td>

(AID)

Aastra Impact Dreams

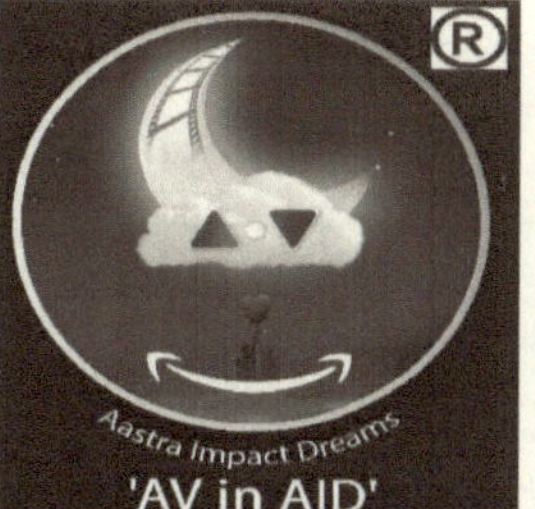

YouTube

@

100% of Author's Earnings

Go to Charity

</td>
</tr>
</table>

PUBLICATIONS
100% of 'AUTHOR EARNINGS' Goto CHARITY

a	COVER	TITLE	Books
		1. **The Real Deal** *(All You Need to Know about Investing in Real Estate)* Genre: Real Estate investing	
		2. **Nuggets of Wisdom** *(Invest in Real Estate with Wisdom)* Genre: Investments	
		3. **Buddha On Wall-Street** *(Knowledge Wisdom Moksha Bliss)* Genre: Finance and Philosophy	
		4. **You Better Watch Out!** *(Technology Change Society Culture)* Genre: Technology & Culture	

PUBLICATIONS
100% of 'AUTHOR EARNINGS' Goto CHARITY

a	COVER	TITLE	Books
	THE ART OF PUBLIC GOOD	**5. The Art of Public Good** *(Power Wisdom Prosperity Balance)* Genre: Public Policy	
	Facets Poetry for All Seasons	**6. FACETS** *(Poetry for all Seasons)* Genre: Poetry & Songs	
	THE POWER OF LOVE	**7. The Power of Love** *(Love Happiness Contentment Bliss)* Genre: Love & Humanity	
	THE G-FORCES	**8. The G-Forces** *(Gita Governance Goodness Godliness)* Genre: Self-Improvement	

PUBLICATIONS
100% of 'AUTHOR EARNINGS' Goto CHARITY

a	COVER	TITLE	Books
		9. The Mind of Champions *(Where Fire & Ice are Forged)* Genre: Self Improvement	
		10. The Edge *(Prepare Plan Execute Win)* Genre: Entrepreneurship	
		11. Hopscotch *(Poetry for all Reasons)* Genre: Poetry & Songs	
		12. Pepper Bright - I *(Snippet of an Adventure)* Genre: Biography	

www.ingramcontent.com/pod-product-compliance
Lightning Source LLC
LaVergne TN
LVHW041016150826
845672LV00001B/110

* 9 7 9 8 8 9 6 3 2 7 7 5 2 *